# Making Practical
# BACKYARD PROJECTS IN WOOD

*Beautiful Things to Make in a Weekend,*
*Including Ready-to-Use Plans & Patterns*

FOX CHAPEL
PUBLISHING

© 2025 Fox Chapel Publishing Company, Inc.

*Making Practical Backyard Projects in Wood* is an original work, first published in 2025 by Fox Chapel Publishing Company, Inc. The patterns contained herein are copyrighted by the authors. Readers may make copies of these patterns for personal use. The patterns themselves, however, are not to be duplicated for resale or distribution under any circumstances. Any such copying is a violation of copyright law.

ISBN 978-1-4971-0508-9

The Cataloging-in-Publication Data is on file with the Library of Congress.

To learn more about the other great books from Fox Chapel Publishing, or to find a retailer near you, call toll-free 800-457-9112, send mail to 903 Square Street, Mount Joy, PA 17552, or visit us at *www.FoxChapelPublishing.com.*

We are always looking for talented authors. To submit an idea, please send a brief inquiry to acquisitions@foxchapelpublishing.com.

Printed in the USA
First printing

# Making Practical
# BACKYARD
# PROJECTS
# IN WOOD

## *Beautiful Things to Make in a Weekend, Including Ready-to-Use Plans & Patterns*

# Table of Contents

**22**

**36**

**44**

**48**

**56**

**62**

**80**

**90**

# Introduction

There's nothing like coming home to an outdoor space that's relaxing and full of wildlife. With the projects in this book, you can look forward to both. Start small with an herb box you can place right on the porch—and some easy plant markers to go with it. Then, make your yard a pollinator's paradise with a DIY insect hotel, bird bath, bat box, bird feeder, and bird house. If you're into bigger builds, you can construct everything from a potato planter and rainwater harvester to an attractive toolshed and Adirondack chair. We even threw in a few decorative designs for fun, like a gnome door.

The best part about these projects is that you don't need years of woodworking experience to be successful; each one includes directions, high-quality photography, and detailed materials lists to help you on your way. Whatever you choose to make, you'll be one step closer to creating a more eco-friendly, beautiful, and welcoming space for you and the creatures you share it with.

Enjoy!

# Tools & Safety

The projects in this book range from small yard accents to large structures, but they all have a few tools in common. If you don't already have a basic tool kit—or if the components have been scattered over the years—save time and frustration by collecting these tools in a bag or bin before you start your first project. You probably already own most of them, but if you need to invest in one or two, rest assured you will use them regularly for years to come.

- **Hammer:** This is an essential tool to any workshop.

- **Screwdrivers/drill with screwdriver bits:** For the sake of ease and convenience, we recommend a cordless drill. Most outdoor screws have a Phillips head, but some are a combination of Phillips and Robertson (square-drive) head. Avoid slotted screws, if possible.

- **Pliers:** Regular; needle-nose.

- **Marking tools:** Pencil and sharpener; black marker. If you plan to work with dark wood, such as teak, mechanical pencils with white lead are available at most fabric stores.

- **Measuring tools and straight edges:** Ruler; tape measure. Try square for smaller projects; carpenter's square for larger projects. A combination square (optional) allows you to adjust the length of the ruler side to fit into tighter areas or for marking distances and to draw lines at a 45-degree angle.

- **Clamps:** Spring clamps; bar clamps. Web clamps are useful for holding irregularly shaped projects.

- **Adjustable wrench:** An essential tool for any workshop, the adjustable wrench can be used to tighten or loosen nuts and bolts of various sizes. Its adjustable jaw allows it to grip onto different widths, making it incredibly versatile for woodworking projects involving metal fasteners.

- **Level:** Crucial for ensuring your projects are perfectly horizontal or vertical, a level is used to check the alignment and flatness of surfaces. It's indispensable when you need to guarantee that your work, from shelving to frames, is precisely even and balanced.

Having the right tools at your fingertips will ensure successful completion of any outdoor project.

- **Cutting tools:** Scissors; wire cutters; razor blade.
- **Adhesives:** Wood glue; blue painter's tape; clear packaging tape; spray adhesive.

A dust mask, hearing protection, and eye protection are essential when working with wood.

# Safety

Whenever you use power tools, there is a chance of injury—anything from dust in your eye to serious cuts. Follow the manufacturer's instructions, use common sense, and heed these precautions to keep yourself safe:

- **Wear safety glasses:** When you're cutting, drilling, or even driving screws and nails, there is a chance of material flying off and hitting you in the eye. Safety glasses protect your eyes from flying debris and dust.

- **Use a dust mask:** Inhaling enough wood dust can injure your lungs, and the dust from varieties of wood that resist decay can be harmful even in small quantities. For small jobs, wear a disposable dust mask. If you're cutting or sanding a lot of wood, invest in a respirator-type mask to filter out even the smallest particles.

- **Protect your ears:** Experts say that exposure to noise as loud as a blender for more than 30 seconds can damage your hearing. Many shop tools—circular saw, jigsaw, table saw, and even a sander—exceed this threshold. Wear earplugs or earmuffs to protect your hearing.

- **Wear gloves:** Heavy-duty gloves will protect your hands and help you avoid splinters, and latex or rubber gloves will keep your hands clean during finishing. **Do not** wear gloves when operating machinery that may snag the glove, as this can result in serious injury.

# PROJECTS:
# Birds, Bats, Bees & Butterflies

# Stylish Birdhouse

*BY BARRY MCKENZIE*

With its classically shingled roof and brilliant, stylized chip carving, you might be hesitant to hang this birdhouse outdoors. But the project is weather resistant, and returning songbirds will reward your generosity with their cheerful presence.

The birdhouse is fairly simple to construct. The bottom of the house has a gate hook to keep the hinged front from being opened by a predator or pushed out by too much nesting material inside. The roof is at a 12-degree slope for water run-off, and the shingles, while easy to carve, make an impressive display.

Use basswood, butternut, or white cedar; more dense wood is difficult to chip carve. The dimensions of this project will change if you use wood thinner than ¾" (1.9cm).

**Tools and Materials**

- Pencil
- Chip carving knife
- Gouge of choice
- Ruler
- Assorted paintbrushes
- Basswood, ¾" (1.9cm) thick: bottom, 4" x 5" (10.2 x 12.7cm) (A)
- Basswood, ¾" (1.9cm) thick: rear, 5" x 8 ¹⁵⁄₁₆" (12.7 x 22.7cm) (B)
- Basswood, ¾" (1.9cm) thick: front, 5" x 7⅞" (12.7 x 24.5cm) (C)
- Basswood, ¾" (1.9cm) thick: sides, 5½" x 8 ¹⁵⁄₁₆" (64.8 x 22.7cm) (D), top angles from 7⅞" (20cm) up to 8 ¹⁵⁄₁₆" (22.7cm)
- Basswood, ¾" (1.9cm) thick: roof, 7" x 8 ¹⁵⁄₁₆" (17.8 x 129.4cm) (E)
- Wooden dowel, ¼"–⁵⁄₁₆" (6–8mm)-dia.: 2 each 1" (2.5cm) long, (F); Do not glue in place
- Gatehook set: 2" (5.1cm) long
- Glue: exterior weather-resistant
- Dark acrylic paint of choice
- Finish, such as exterior spar urethane
- Graphite paper

The hinged front panel opens for easy cleaning and secures with a simple gate hook.

## CONSTRUCTION NOTES

- Drill holes for dowels at least ½" (1.3cm) deep.
- Place the two hinge dowels in the front piece before assembling.
- The dowels can be up to ⁵⁄₁₆" (8mm) dia.
- To accommodate the latch, the sides are not flush with the bottom part (A).
- The top of the front piece (C) has rounded edges to clear the underside of the roof when you swing it open.

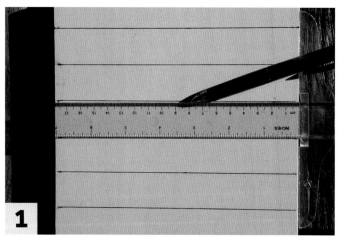

**1. Divide the roof into rows.** Draw six horizontal lines, 1" (2.5cm) apart, across the width of the roof to make seven rows of shingles. Make a deep stop cut along these lines with a chip carving knife. The cuts should be between 1/16" (2mm) and 1/8" (3mm) deep.

**2. Taper the shingles.** Use a gouge of your choice to remove wood up to the vertical cuts made in Step 1. Taper the shingles so it looks like the lower shingle disappears beneath the edge of the one above it. Feel free to deepen the stop cut as you go. Work across each row before moving on to the next. The depth is up to you.

**3. Divide the rows into shingles.** Each row of shingles is staggered in relation to the row above it. Start with a shingle width of about 3/4" (1.9cm), and vary the width from there. Do not make every shingle the same width. Cut along these lines with the chip carving knife to divide the rows into individual shingles.

**4. Outline the thickness of the shingles.** Carve a line along the bottom and sides of the shingles to represent the thickness. This gives the illusion that each shingle is individually carved. Since each row is tapered, it will look like the individual shingles are tapered. Do not sand the shingles smooth.

**5. Mount the gate hook.** Screw the eyelet into the front (C) just below the bottom (A). Do not screw the eyelet in completely; that way, you can adjust the fit of the hook after you attach it to the bottom (A). Screw the hook in place, and test the fit. If the hook fits loosely, tighten the eyelet screwed into the front (C) until the hook holds tightly.

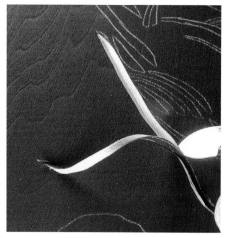

**6**

## CHIP TIP

The type of chip carving in this project is called "stylized freeform," which is not as precise as geometric chip carving. Chip carving through paint does have a tendency to dull the knife's cutting edge a little faster, so I strop more often. You could easily carve the design in shallow relief, if desired.

**6. Chip carve the design.** Transfer the design to the painted birdhouse using light-colored graphite paper. Cut along one side of the pattern line, angling the knife in so the cut ends at the center of the chip to be removed. Flip the birdhouse around and cut in toward the center from the other side to free the chip. Make sure the lines are smooth and even.

## BIRDHOUSE BASICS

- I didn't add a perch because predators tend to use the perch more often than the songbirds. I have seen nesting birds fly straight into the hole and exit the same way.

- The location of the birdhouse should be as far as 100 feet away from other competitive birds. Even self-nesting birds will be harassed by a bluebird if they are using a birdhouse nearby.

- Clean out the birdhouse in early spring before the migrating birds return. Before opening the birdhouse, make sure nobody has taken up residence. I have seen several bluebirds share a birdhouse over a mild winter. I also have one flying squirrel that has made a permanent home in one of my birdhouses. It was a big surprise to both of us when I tried to clean out the bedding material and found a wide-eyed flying squirrel looking back at me!

| BIRDHOUSE SPECIFICATIONS FOR DIFFERENT SPECIES | | |
|---|---|---|
| **Bird Species** | **Entrance Hole** | **Mounting Height** |
| Chickadee | 1⅛" (2.9cm)-dia. | 6' (1.8cm) |
| Tufted Titmouse, Nuthatch | 1¼" (3.2cm)-dia. | 6' (1.8cm) |
| Blue Bird, House Wren | 1½" (3.8cm)-dia. | 6' (1.8cm) |
| Swallow | 1½" (3.8cm)-dia. | 10' (3m) |
| House Finch | 2" (5.1cm)-dia. | 8' (2.4m) |
| Purple Martin | 2½" (6.4cm)-dia. | 15' (4.6m) |

# Bird Feeder

*BY JON DECK*

Any time is a great time to provide wild birds much-needed nutrition as natural supplies grow scarce. With four seed hoppers, this feeder holds a large amount of food for winter feeding, and lets you offer a variety of seed mixes to attract more species to your backyard year-round.

This project requires basic scrolling skills, but the woodworking aspects can be a bit of a challenge. It's important that the components are measured and cut with care for a good fit during assembly. I recommend cutting all the hopper face layers (plywood, hardboard, and acrylic) on a table saw for accurate panels. The feeder must bear up to the elements, so materials should be rated for exterior use. When called for, allow adequate painting and drying time between those steps before moving on. Plastic milk jugs make perfect seamless seed hoppers and let you recycle in a rather unique way.

All of the ½" (or 1.3cm) plywood parts can be cut from a single 24" by 48" (61cm by 1.2m) sheet. Follow the measured drawing and parts list (page 21) and lay out all your measurements carefully with a square.

## Tools and Materials

- Exterior plywood, ½" (1.3cm) thick: 24" x 48" (61cm x 1.2m)
- Pine, 1x2: 72" (1.8m) long
- Pine, 1x6: 48" (1.2m) long
- Tempered hardboard, ⅛ (3mm) thick: 24" x 48" (61cm x 1.2m)
- Clear acrylic plastic, 2mm thick: 18" x 24" (45.7 x 61cm)
- Plastic jugs: 4 each, one gallon
- Dowels: ³⁄₁₆" (5mm)-dia. x 18" (45.7cm), ½" (1.3cm)-dia. x 48" (1.2m)
- Large wooden finial
- Screws, exterior: 1¼", 2½" (3.2, 6.4cm)
- Screws, lath: ⁹⁄₁₆" (1.4cm)
- Nails, 18 gauge: ⅝", 1¼" (1.6, 3.2cm)
- Glue: exterior wood, cyanoacrylate (CA)
- Wood filler, exterior
- Caulk, exterior silicone: clear
- Sandpaper: 120, 220 grit
- Spray adhesive: temporary-bond
- Tape: blue painter's, clear packaging
- Paint, exterior: spray and/or brushable
- Spar varnish: clear spray
- Rare earth magnets, rectangular: 8 each 2mm-thick
- Hinges, narrow: 4 pair 1"
- Tape measure
- Steel rule or straightedge
- Large square
- Scroll saw blades: #5 skip-tooth
- Saws: table, miter
- Drill with bits: ¹⁄₁₆" (2mm), ⅛" (3mm), ³⁄₁₆" (5mm) dia. twist, #2 Phillips head
- Nail gun: 18-gauge finish
- Screwdriver
- Caulking gun
- Clamps: assorted
- Utility knife
- Kitchen shears
- Paintbrush

**1. Cut out the section supports (A).** Use a scroll saw. For one, make a slot from the top, and for the other, from the bottom. Draw a pencil line ¼" (6.4mm) from the right and left edges on both sides of each support. Set the scroll saw to 45 degrees and cut a bevel on the four marked edges to form the outside corners of the feeder. Make these bevels on both supports. Cut the tray (B) on a table saw.

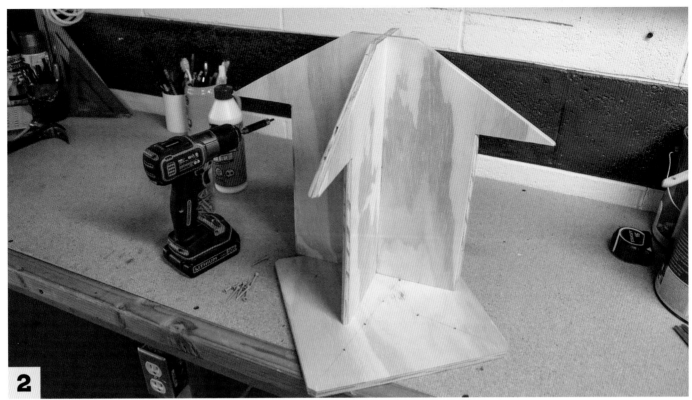

**2**

**2. Slide the two section supports together.** It should be a snug fit. Mark the tray with a line from corner to corner and drill ⅛" (3mm)-diameter holes to mount the section supports. Be sure one hole is dead center on the tray. After drilling, cut ¼" (6.4mm) off the points on all four corners of the tray with the scroll saw to provide drain holes. Apply glue to the bottom of the section support assembly. Starting with the center hole, from the underside, mount the assembly onto the tray where the two supports cross with 1¼" (32mm)-long screws. Align the supports with the pencil lines and add the remaining screws.

**3**

**3. Cut the roof supports (C) to size.** Make eight blanks. Draw a pencil line ⁵⁄₁₆" (8mm) in from the edge of each blank. Set the scroll saw at a 25-degree angle, and cut the smaller section off the blank. Align the angled blank with the section support so the angle meets the roofline from the flat, top portion down to the gable end. Holding the blank in position, run a pencil across the end of the blank along the bottom of the gable. Cut the waste off the end of the roof support. Mark and cut the roof supports, one at a time. The angles will be opposite on the companion side of the gable, so it is easier to do than keeping each individual angle straight.

**5. Paint the bird feeder assembly.** Use a good exterior paint. Also paint the tray sides and roof cap. Because I used a high gloss paint, I masked the areas that will glue together with painter's tape. Painted surfaces don't accept glue as well as bare wood. Allow the paint to dry completely before assembling.

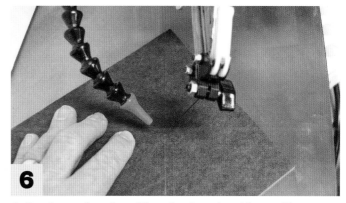

**4. Glue and clamp the roof supports in place.** Let the glue dry. Repeat with each gable. Measure and cut the roof cap (D). Cut the tray sides (F1, F2) to length with a miter saw. Sand the roof cap, tray sides, and bird feeder assembly to prepare for painting.

**6. Cut the roof sections (E) to size.** I used a table saw. Measure and mark the gable ends on the blanks using the measured drawing on page 102. Set the scroll saw to 25° and undercut a bevel along the lines you've just drawn.

**7. Add the roof cap to the feeder.** Drill a ⅛" (3mm)-diameter hole in the center of the roof cap and the top of the assembly where the two support sections meet. Apply glue to the top of the assembly and, using a small nail, align the roof cap through the drilled holes. Be sure the corners of the roof cap align with the gables, and tack the roof cap in place with 1¼" (3.2cm)-long nails.

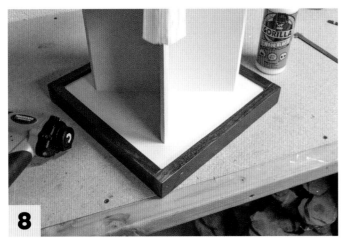

**8. Add the tray sides.** Set the assembly on a scrap of ¾" (1.9cm) plywood just smaller than the tray. This lifts the tray so you can position the sides properly. Apply glue to the edges of the tray and position the tray sides—short sides (F1) and long sides (F2) on opposite ends. Tack the tray sides onto the tray with 1 ¼" (3.2cm)-long nails. This assembly should set drain holes in each corner of the tray.

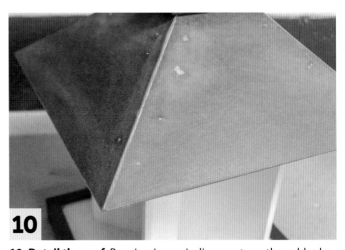

**9. Dry-fit the roof sections (E).** Tape three roof sections together along their gable ends with painter's tape. Drape the sections over the assembly, sliding the sections up under the roof cap. Slide the fourth roof section in place and check the fit of the entire roof. When satisfied with the fit, run a bead of caulk down the gable and add wood glue to the gable supports. Return the roof sections as you did in the dry-fit, and tack them in place with ⅝" (1.6cm)-long nails.

**10. Detail the roof.** Repair minor misalignments on the gables by trimming with a utility knife, adding wood putty, and sanding. Fill nail holes with wood putty. This is mainly for cosmetics—the caulk under the gables will keep rain out of your feeder. When finished, paint the roof with exterior paint.

**11. Cut blanks for the face frames (G), face panels (H), and hopper windows (I).** Use the table saw. Stack the materials to cut all four face frames and hopper windows at once. Sandwich the acrylic plastic between the wood pieces. Apply a pattern to the stack, and cut the seed slot. Unstack, remove the acrylic plastic, and restack the face frames. Drill a blade-entry hole, and cut the face frame opening.

**12. Stack face panel blanks in pairs, with the smooth side up.** Apply the songbird pattern to one stack, and the cardinal pattern to the other stack. Drill blade-entry holes and cut the panels. When finished, sand the panels and face frames, and glue them together. Paint the assemblies and let them dry. Remove the film from one side of the hopper windows and mount it to the backside of the face panel with cyanoacrylate (CA) glue. Note: Be sure the seed slots all line up before gluing.

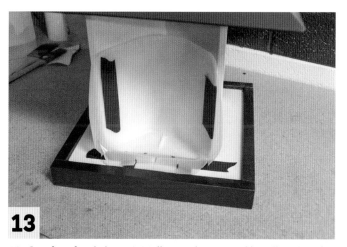

**13. Cut the plastic jugs.** Initially, cut the top and handle side off with a kitchen shears. Place the jug in the feeder and mark the jug where the corners, front edge, and seed slot of the hopper section are located with painter's tape. *Note: All the hopper frames are offset, so the left side of the frame aligns with the corner of the section support.* Crease the plastic along the tape to form a flange. Trim the bottom corners of the jug to fit the hopper frame, but leave a flange to mount to the bottom of the frame. Repeat for all of the hoppers.

**14. Remove the remaining film from the acrylic plastic.** Place the hopper frame face down on a padded surface. Position the hopper and drill three ⅛" (3mm)-diameter pilot holes on each side flange and one on both sides of the seed slot. Run a bead of silicone caulk down each side and along the bottom of the frame. Place the hopper in position and secure with ⁹⁄₁₆" (1.4cm)-long lath screws in each pilot hole. Fill any gaps in the corners with silicone caulk. Repeat for the other hoppers.

**16. Cut the perches (M) and supports (N) to length.** Measure in 1½" (3.8cm) from the end of each perch and drill a ³⁄₁₆" (5mm) by ⅜" (1cm)-deep hole. Make sure the holes align with each other. Glue the perch supports into these holes. Apply spar varnish to these assemblies. Paint the finial and let everything dry.

**15. Place a hopper with the left side of the frame aligned with the corner of the section support.** Position a hinge on both sides of the seed slot, 1" (2.5cm) from the opening. Drill ¹⁄₁₆" (2mm)-diameter pilot holes in the frame and the tray. Add the screws to secure the hopper. Repeat for all of the hoppers.

**17. Add the perches.** Drill two ³⁄₁₆" (5mm)-diameter mounting holes in each tray side. Glue the perches in place keeping an equal distance from the tray on all sides. Cut the frame edge trim (J), and paint it to match the face frames. When dry, glue them to the outside right edge of each face frame for a finished look. Screw the finial into the hole in the roof cap.

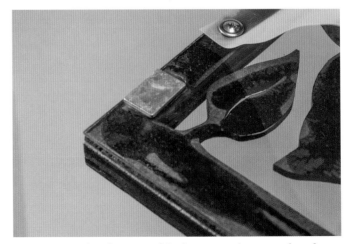

**18. Mount the magnets.** Glue a rare earth magnet to each section support corner, and each corner of the hopper so they meet for a firm closure. Use CA glue.

**19. Mount the magnets.** Glue a rare earth magnet to each section support corner, and each corner of the hopper so they meet for a firm closure. Use CA glue.

| | Part | Qty. | Materials | Dimensions | Presentation |
|---|---|---|---|---|---|
| | **BIRD FEEDER PARTS LIST** | | | | |
| A | Section support | 2 | Plywood, ½" (or 1.3cm) thick | 14" x 18½" (35.6 x 47cm) | Drawing |
| B | Tray | 1 | Plywood, ½" (or 1.3cm) thick | 11" (27.9cm) square | Dimensions |
| C | Roof support | 8 | Pine, ¾" (1.9cm) thick | ¾" x 8½" (1.9 x 21.6cm) | Dimensions |
| D | Roof cap | 1 | Pine, ¾" (1.9cm) thick | 4¼" (10.8cm) square | Dimensions |
| E | Roof section | 4 | Hardboard, ⅛" (3mm) thick | 6⅝" x 13¾" (16.8 x 34.9cm) | Drawing |
| F1 | Tray side, short | 2 | Pine, ¾" (1.9cm) thick | 1½" x 11" (3.8 x 27.9cm) | Dimensions |
| F2 | Tray side, long | 2 | Pine, ¾" (1.9cm) thick | 1½" x 12½" (3.8 x 31.8cm) | Dimensions |
| G | Face frame | 4 | Plywood, ½" (or 1.3cm) thick | 8⁵⁄₁₆" x 9½" (21.1 x 24.1cm) | Pattern |
| H | Face panel | 4 | Hardboard, ⅛" (3mm) thick | 8⁵⁄₁₆" x 9½" (21.1 x 24.1cm) | Pattern |
| I | Hopper window | 4 | Acrylic plastic sheet, 2mm thick | 8⁵⁄₁₆" x 9½" (21.1 x 24.1cm) | Dimensions |
| J | Frame edge trim | 4 | Hardboard, ⅛" (3mm) thick | ¾" x 9½" (1.9 x 24.1cm) | Dimensions |
| K | Hopper | 4 | Plastic milk jug | One gallon | |
| L | Bracket | 4 | Pine, ¾" (1.9cm) thick | 5½" x 6½" (14 x 16.5cm) | Pattern |
| M | Perch | 4 | Dowel, ½" (1.2cm)-dia. | 12" (30.5cm) long | Dimensions |
| N | Perch support | 8 | Dowel, ³⁄₁₆" (5mm)-dia. | 1¾" (4.4cm) long | Dimensions |

# Bat Box

*BY PAUL MEISEL, STEPHEN MOSS, AND
ALAN AND GILL BRIDGEWATER*

This bat box is a winner on many counts. The bark is left intact so
the box is perfectly camouflaged. It's made from easy-to-work-with
green wood with interior surfaces that are rough-sawn and gouge-
textured, providing good footholds for pups or nestlings. The whole
project can be assembled quickly and easily.

When you are searching for wood, do your best to select sound
slabs of hardwood with the bark still firmly attached. If the wood
is in any way flawed—long splits, spongy areas, pierced with large
insect holes—it's best to look around for another piece.

## THE DESIGN 〉〉〉〉〉〉〉〉〉〉〉

The clever thing about this design is the way the back slab is cut and
worked so that the front and roof slabs notch together, allowing
the rain to run down and off the box without entering it. The bark
on the front of the box runs from top to bottom, making it almost
invisible when it's mounted on a tree. Perhaps most importantly
of all, in view of the concerns about declining wood resources,
the design uses first-cut sawmill wood that would otherwise go
to waste.

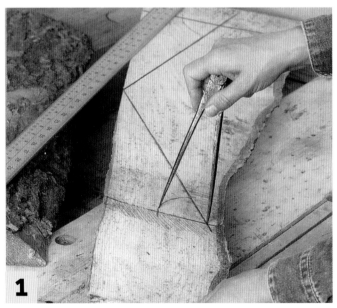

**1. Lay out the wood.** Use a pencil, ruler, square, and dividers to lay
out the measurements on the sawn face of the wood. Do your best
to avoid deep knotholes, twisted grain, and splits.

**2. Cut out the pieces.** Use a band saw. Keep in mind that
you will have to cut the wood with the bark face on the
underside (meaning the blade will snatch), so you must be
extra careful to keep your fingers well away from the front of
the blade. You will need help with the larger boards.

**3. Finish cutting the pieces to size.** Use a log saw. Run the two stop-cut notches halfway through the 1⅜" (35mm) thickness of the backboard (A). Aim to finish up with the bottom of the cuts parallel to the back sawn face of the wood.

**4. Cut the backboard notches.** Use a mallet and 1¼" (32mm) straight gouge to remove the waste between the two stop cut notches. Hold the gouge at a low angle. Start at the center and work through to the end, so that the length of the gouge stroke is controlled by the stop cut. Clear the waste from one end, and then turn the wood around and repeat the procedure for the other end.

**5. Fit the side boards.** Dry assemble the components. Then, when you're satisfied with the fit, nail the two side boards (C) firmly into place on the backboard, using a cross-peen hammer and 2" (51mm) nails.

**6. Complete the assembly.** When you are satisfied with the appearance of the structure, go over the whole box, adding more nails for stability as needed.

## INSTALLING THE BAT BOX

Choose a suitable tree and position the box about 8'–16' (2.5m–5m) above the ground, with the side entrance holes in a sheltered spot. Unlike with most bird boxes, this nest box should be situated so that it receives plenty of sunlight. (Mother bats need a warm environment in which to raise their pups in the spring.) Using a claw hammer, attach the box firmly in place with 3" (76mm) nails at the top and bottom. Take special care when installing the bat box, as a fall from a tree can be dangerous. Use a sturdy ladder and ask a partner to hold it steady while you attach the box.

## BATS OR BIRDS YOU'LL ATTRACT

Biologically speaking, bats are not birds but mammals: they have noses instead of beaks and fur instead of feathers, and they give birth to live (hairless) babies, called "pups" —only one to three a year—rather than laying eggs. But like birds, they are lightweight, can use their wings to fly, and use nests to raise their young.

If you are fortunate enough to spot bats swirling in your yard at dusk, you can take comfort knowing they are devouring mosquitoes at the insatiable rate of hundreds per hour. In addition, bats also eat garden pests, including cucumber beetles and June bugs, and support plant diversity by spreading seeds in their guano. The idea of this box is to make it look as much like the natural nesting site of the bat as possible.

In addition to bats, this nest box may attract the American treecreeper, which generally nests in tiny cracks and crevices beneath the bark. The treecreeper will use twigs, stems, roots, and bark to conceal its nest.

Big Brown Bat *(Eptesicus fuscus)*

Eastern Red Bat *(Lasiurus borealis)*

Little Brown Bat *(Myotis lucifugus)*

American Treecreeper *(Certhia americana)*

# Japanese Birdbath

*BY PAUL MEISEL, STEPHEN MOSS, AND ALAN AND GILL BRIDGEWATER*

This project draws its inspiration from the calming imagery of traditional Japanese Zen gardens. The monolithic block of wood mounted on a tree stump takes on much the same role as the Japanese sentinel or "guardian stone." The carved ripples on the surface of the wood symbolize waves, and the attractive hollow filled with water makes for a perfect birdbath.

It is vital to pick an easy-to-carve wood. We chose a slab of straight-grained, knot-free English lime, but you could use basswood or aromatic cedar. When you are selecting a slab of wood, make sure that it is well-seasoned—meaning the wood has been allowed to dry for at least a year.

This is an especially good project for those new to woodcarving, as it teaches basic gouge cuts. Because there's so much wood to work with, a slip of the tool can be easily covered up in later stages.

**Tools and Materials**

- Pencil
- Felt-tip marker
- Ruler
- Straightedge
- Power drill with bits: 1" (25mm), 2" (51mm) dia. Forstner
- Adze
- Wooden mallets: heavyweight, lightweight
- Straight gouges: 1" (25mm) and 1½" (38mm)
- Bent gouge: 1" (25mm)
- V-tool of choice
- Lime or wood of choice, 6" (15.2cm) thick: 23¼" x 30" (59.1 x 76.2cm) (A)
- Tree section, about 18" (45.7cm) thick: 16" (40.6cm)-dia. (B)
- Tracing pape

## THE DESIGN )))))))))))))

While in many ways this is the simplest of projects—not much more than a slab of wood with a carved hollow—the actual size and weight of the wood does make for difficulties. The wood is heavy, so it doesn't need to be held or clamped. Simply set the slab on the ground, and then move around it as you carve to complete your work.

This design is practical and sturdy, as well as being a very attractive piece of garden furniture. Birds come in all shapes and sizes, so a birdbath needs to have a "shallow end" and a "deep end" to accommodate a wide variety.

**1. Lay out the design.** Trace out the design at full size. With a pencil, press-transfer the traced lines through to the face of the wood. Establish the center of the hollow and use a straightedge and felt-tip marker to rule lines that radiate out from the center.

**2. Drill out the waste.** Remember that the hollow needs to be deepest at the narrow end. Use the drill to clear the bulk of the waste. Start with a 2" (51mm)-dia. Forstner bit for boring out the widest and deepest holes, and then follow up with a 1" (25mm)-dia. bit.

**3. Rough out with an adze and gouge.** Use an adze to cut down to the depth of the drilled holes. Hold the adze at a fairly flat angle, and then work from the drawn line through to the center. Be careful not to sink the blade too deeply. With the mallets and a 1½" (38mm) straight gouge of your choice, smooth out the deepest part of the hollow.

**4. Refine the bowl.** Use a 1" (25mm) straight gouge to establish the edge of the hollow—you need a nice, clean, smooth curve—and skim the surface to a smooth finish with a bent gouge of your choice. Work with smaller and smaller strokes until you achieve a fine, ripple-textured finish.

**5**

**5. Cut the V-grooves.** Hold a V-tool at a low angle and work from the edge of the hollow toward the edge of the wood, creating smooth, relatively consistent rays all the way around the hollow. Be very careful not to dig too deeply into the wood. Continue until the pattern of grooves completely covers the surface. Do not apply a finish to this project, as it could harm the birds.

## SETTING UP THE BIRDBATH

Ideally, your birdbath should be situated in an open area to minimize the chances of cats sneaking up on the birds as they wash or drink. Keep the bath filled on a daily basis, maybe more frequently in hot weather. Every week or so, give your birdbath a thorough cleaning (you can use household cleaners, but rinse the bath thoroughly afterward to remove any trace of chemicals). In harsh winter weather, make sure the water doesn't freeze by topping it off with warm water from time to time.

When you have selected a suitable site—preferably within view of your house and well away from prowling cats and noisy children—set the tree stump (B) in place, check that it is firm and level, and then get help to lift the slab (A) into position.

## BIRDS YOU'LL ATTRACT

Depending on where you live, you might attract the above birds and many more! A well-made birdbath is one of the essential ingredients in creating a bird-friendly garden, giving winged visitors a regular source of clean water to drink and bathe in.

Most birds bathe at least once a day, generally in the morning or evening. Bathing is vital for birds to keep their plumage clean and their feathers in tip-top condition. It is especially important in the winter, as it allows them to fluff out their feathers properly to insulate themselves against the cold. As natural sources of water, such as lakes and ponds, may be some distance away, many birds depend on water sources provided by humans, either in the form of birdbaths or garden ponds.

Eastern Bluebird *(Sialia sialis)*

Northern Cardinal
*(Cardinalis cardinalis)*

Mourning Dove *(Zenaida macroura)*

# Make a Bug Hotel

## Tools and Materials

- Hammer
- Saw
- Drill
- ¹⁄₃₂" (0.8mm) drill bit
- ¼" (6mm) drill bit
- ³⁄₈" (10mm) drill bit
- Small T-square or straightedge
- Ruler or tape measure
- Pencil or black marker
- Two 6" x 6' x 1" (15.2 x 182.9 x 2.5cm) white pine boards, untreated
- 20' (6.1m) of bamboo
- 12" x 6" (30.5 x 15.2cm) log
- A collection of tree bark, pinecones, and small twigs
- 12" (30.5cm) piece of dried log; oak, ash, and beech are good choices
- Forty 1½" (3.8cm) nails

Although bees and bugs are very capable of finding their homes in nature, as they have done for millions of years, bug houses have become more important to help pollinators find a place near their food source. As more land is being developed, bugs and bees are challenged more every year to find a home close to pollinating plants during the spring and summer months.

Giving your pollinators an easy-to-find home within feet of your flowering plants and vegetables is a great way keep pollinators nearby, making life a little easier for our tiny pollinating bugs and bees.

There are many designs for bug houses. No design is better than the other, but to attract a lot of different types of pollinating bees and beetles, a bug house should include a range of natural materials and have different compartments for different types and sizes of insects. This four-compartment bug hotel is made of all-natural materials, requires only a few tools, and can be easily placed against a shed wall, a pole, or a table near your garden.

**1. Measure and cut four pieces of 12" (30.5cm) long pine boards.** These four pieces will make your hotel frame.

**2. Use your pencil to mark three small dots on the right side of all four frame pieces.** Place the dots ½" (1.2cm) from each side, and place one in the middle.

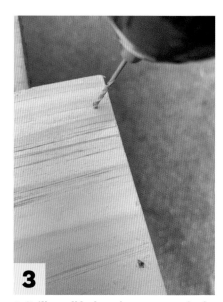

**3. Drill small holes where you marked the wood.**

**4.** Place a nail into each hole.

**5. Using your hammer, pound the nails into the left side end edge of each board.** Repeat until all four pieces are connected. Do not use glues or adhesives, as these can be toxic to insects and bees.

**6. Cut a piece of pine to fit across the inside of the frame.** This will be for your center dividers. To ensure the perfect fit, simply place the board down and draw a small mark on the inside edge. Using your straight edge, draw a line straight across, then cut along it.

**7. On the same board, draw two lines across, spaced 3 ¾" (9.5cm) from each side.** Mark three evenly spaced spots across each line, then drill.

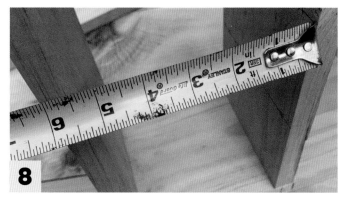

**8. Fit the long divider piece into the frame.** Do not nail it into place. Once placed in, measure the distance between inside of the frame. Measure both sides.

9. **Next, cut two shorter dividers and nail them to your long middle divider.** The middle divider will be placed horizontally. With the fully assembled middle dividers nailed together, slide them into the frame.

10. **Draw straight lines on the outside of the frame where the edges of the dividers meet the frame.** Then, drill three holes through the frame board only, and nail it into place.

11. **With remaining white pine, measure and cut two pieces to cover the back of the frame from side to side.** Drill holes, then nail into place.

**12**

**13**

**12. Measure the inside depth of your bug house and cut bamboo and log pieces to length.** Make sure no pieces stick out of the frame. Then, with a drill, drill different-sized holes using your ⅜" and ¼" (9.5 and 6.4mm) drill bits in the log pieces. Drill about 5" (12.7cm) into the log pieces. Do not drill the entire way through the log.

**13. When you're ready to fill your bug hotel, place the log pieces first.** Surround each piece with bamboo tubes cut to the same length. Fill each compartment until all pieces are tightly against each other. Fill the small compartments with a combination of pinecones, tree bark, and twigs.

## FILLING YOUR BUG HOTEL

When filling your bug hotel, the goal is to provide as many open cavities as possible for bees and bugs to lay eggs and protect themselves from the weather. For this project, we used a collection of small pinecones, tree bark we found on fallen trees in the woods, small branches found on the ground, a piece of an old, dried-out log, and several feet of bamboo. It's important not to cut down live trees or break branches off living plants.

PROJECTS:
# Games
# & Décor

# Backyard Dominoes

*BY COLLEEN PASTOOR*

This giant set of dominoes is a great game for kids and adults alike. My kids play with them more than we do these days, but back when we first made them, my husband had never played an actual game of dominoes before, and he loved it. Whether you use traditional dominoes rules or play one of the other dozens of games you can play with dominoes, these should never get old!

## Tools and Materials

- 1x6 lumber: 28, each 11" (27.9cm) long (cut from four 8' [2.4m] boards)
- Damp cloth
- Pencil
- Stain, such as Minwax®: early American
- Rags
- Rubber gloves
- White indoor/outdoor paint
- Sealer, such as clear spray or wipe-on

**1. Cut the dominoes.** Mark and cut your 1x6 boards into 11" (27.9cm) pieces. The math here is that dominoes should be twice as long as they are wide; accounting for actual lumber size, that works out to 11" (27.9cm) long. You will need 28 pieces total.

**2. Sand.** After cutting, sand each piece. Sanding will give you a beautifully smooth surface and help the stain penetrate more evenly. Wipe the sanded tiles clean of any sawdust with a damp cloth.

**3. Stain.** You can leave your dominoes the natural wood color or stain them as I did (I used the shade Early American by Minwax®). I love the look of white dots on dominoes, and the natural wood just wasn't dark enough for them to show up nicely. Wipe stain onto each tile with a rag (make sure you're wearing gloves), staining one of the sides plus all the edges. Let dry, and then flip and stain the second side.

**4. Paint the dots.** When the stain has cured, paint your domino dots following the guide on page 105. I used a paintbrush, but you could also use a ¾" (1.9cm) spouncer (a round sponge brush for dabbing) to create consistent dots.

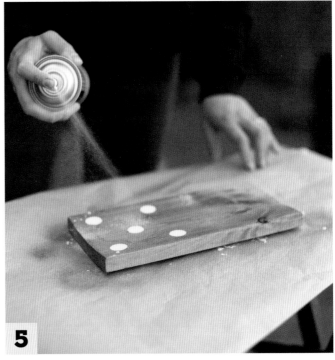

**5. Seal.** After the paint has dried, seal your dominoes. I chose an outdoor-rated spray sealer for ease, but a brush-on or wipe-on sealer would provide more protection if you plan to leave the tiles out exposed to the elements long-term.

# HOW TO PLAY DOMINOES

**Start:** You can play with two to four players, either as individuals or in teams of two. Shuffle the tiles facedown. To determine who goes first, everyone draws a tile. Whoever has the highest double tile starts. If no one drew a double, whoever's tile adds up to the largest total goes first. Shuffle the pile again.

Every player draws a certain number of tiles depending on how many people are playing. With two players, draw seven tiles; with three players, draw five tiles; with four players, draw four tiles. This is your hand. Try to keep your tiles to yourself until you play them.

**Play:** The first player places a single tile in the middle of the game area. Then, going in a circle, each person adds a tile to the game area by matching up one of their tiles with a tile end in the game area that has a same number. So, if you have a tile with three dots on one end, you can match it up to an existing open tile with three dots. (Each dot is called a "pip!")

If you can't match any of the open tile ends, draw a tile from the pile. If you can play it, play it; if you can't, add it to your hand, and it's the end of your turn. (Once no tiles are left in the pile, you simply skip your turn if you can't play a tile from your hand.)

Blank tile ends can either be matched up with other blank tile ends only, or you can decide that they are "wild cards" that can be matched with any other tile. Decide on this before you start playing! Double tiles must be matched up in the center of the existing tile, rather than attached to just one end of the existing tile.

Whoever runs out of tiles first wins the round! When the round is over, everyone who has tiles left in their hand (everyone who didn't win) adds up all the dots on all of their tiles, and then all these numbers are added together. The winner gets awarded these points. For example, in a four-player game, if the three losers of the round each have tiles that add up to five, then the total is 15, and the winner gets awarded 15 points.

**Win:** Whoever reaches 100 points first wins the game!

# Tic-Tac-Toe

*BY FRANK EGHOLM*

*ILLUSTRATIONS BY LILLIAN EGHOLM*

At the school where I used to work, they made large tic-tac-toe games that would lay in the schoolyard for the children, or maybe teachers, to use on their breaks. With this version, you'll have to use some of the interlocking techniques that, on much larger scales, can be found in log cabins and even in the wooden structure of medieval churches and cathedrals. If you want, you can make decorations on the game pieces. To play, each player takes turns placing or moving their game piece. The first to get three in a line is the winner. This project can be carved by a child with adult supervision.

## Tools and Materials

- Markers, paint, leather, glue, small drill bit (optional)
- Carving knife
- Coping saw or folding saw
- Pruning shears
- Straight, green branches, ¾" (1.9cm)-dia.: game board, 4 each 18" (45.7cm) long
- Straight, green branches, ½" (1.3cm)-dia.: Xs, 8 each 4¾" (12.1cm) long
- Twine or string
- Thin, bendable branches, like willow stems: Os, 4 each
- Straight, green branches, ¾" (2cm)-dia.: alternative figures, 2" (5.1cm) long (optional)

## HELPFUL CARVING TECHNIQUES

**Thumb technique:** This is one of the most useful techniques. It is very safe, and you can use a lot of force. The thumb on the hand holding the wood is supporting the back of the knife blade. This thumb acts as a cantilever point and is not pushing the blade forward. Instead, you are pulling the handle backward and cutting with the tip of the blade. Your thumb might become sore, but you can use a thumb protector, like a fingertip from a thick garden glove, to prevent this. In the beginning, this technique might be difficult to learn, but all of a sudden you will get it, and it will be worth it.

**Potato peeler/end-grain technique:** The knife is held as shown. The hand is pulled back and makes small cuts. It is safer to use the base of the blade than the tip. If you can "hide" your thumb under the branch, this is safer. Take it slow and familiarize yourself with the technique and it will be very useful.

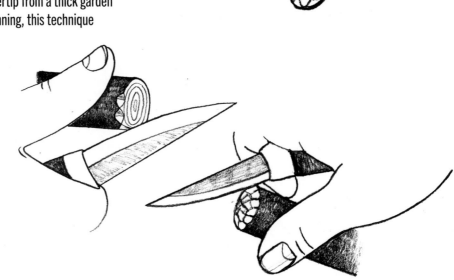

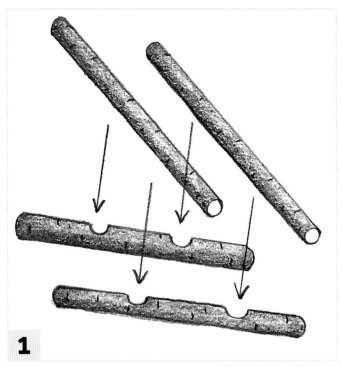

**1. Carve notches.** Carve two notches in two of the long branches, 6" (15.2cm) from each end and deep enough that the other branches can be laid across them. Use the thumb technique and turn the branch frequently so you cut from each side and always away from yourself.

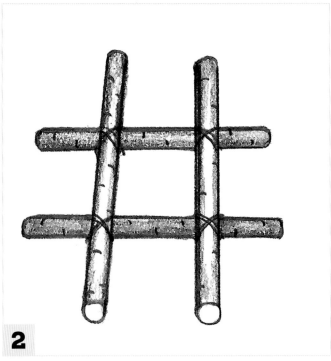

**2. Construct the game board.** Lash the four long branches together with twine.

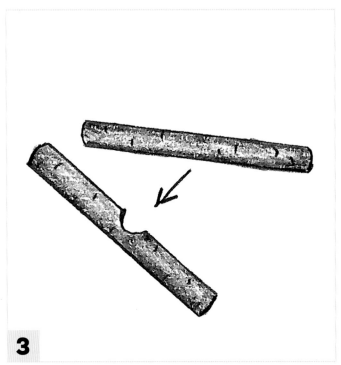

**3. Make the Xs.** Cut a notch in the middle of three of the shorter branches, and then tie another branch with twine to it so they form an X.

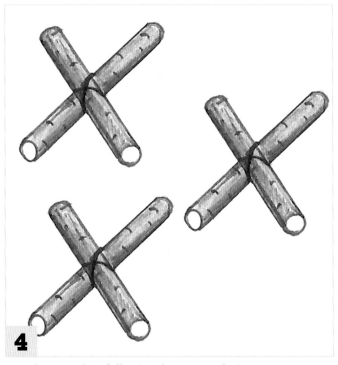

**4. Make several Xs, following the same technique.**

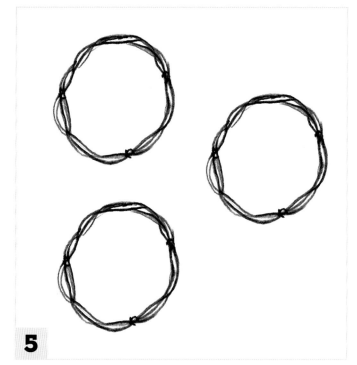

**5**

**5. Make the Os.** Make several rings with the bendable branches. Make a ring, and then wind the rest of the branch around the ring. If necessary, you can tie the end with a bit of string so the ring doesn't unwind.

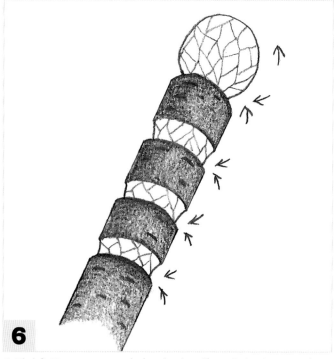

**6**

**6. Finish.** To carve a rounded end, take off small shavings, turning the branch a bit each time. First make the end pointy, and then round off the rest. Carve the optional notches for added flair. To make the notches, use the thumb technique and turn the branch, carving in from both sides if possible. You might have to tighten the string once the branches dry up. Challenge a friend or loved one to a round (or several) of tic-tac-toe.

## TIC-TAC-TOE WITH FIGURES

If you want a fun alternative to the Xs and Os, you can substitute two sets of figures. Carve them in the ends of the branches and cut them off with the saw. They have to be around 2" (5.1cm) tall.

**Hearts.** Begin by carving the branch narrower, as shown. Then carve out the heart shape. At the top where you have to carve the small notch, carve in toward the center from both sides to remove a small chip. You will have to carve against yourself, so take care and only take off tiny shavings at a time.

**Dogs.** Round off the end of a branch. Draw on the dog's face with a marker. Drill holes for the ears and cut ears from thin leather. Add a little bit of glue to the holes and push in the ends of the ears with a tiny stick.

Your choice! Try to come up with your own figures.

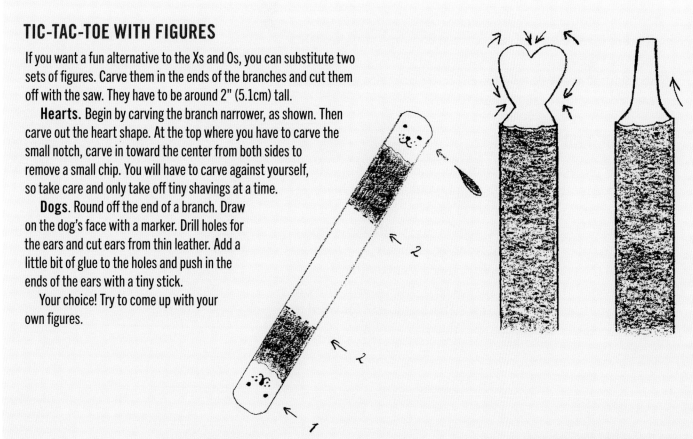

# Gnome Door

*BY OJARS PLISIS*

This fun and whimsical door uses inexpensive materials found at most home improvement stores. It takes about an hour to complete, but thanks to a waterproof glue bond and polyurethane seal, this door will stand up to the elements for years.

This project uses BCX plywood that comes in larger sheets in ¼" (6mm) and ½" (12mm) thicknesses. You'll be using only a small portion of each, so there will be plenty left over for future projects.

## MAKING THE PROJECT

Apply the patterns to the blanks with spray adhesive. Cut the arch (inside and out) on a scroll saw and use this as a tracing pattern for the door and backing. Trace around the outside for the backing, and then trace inside for the door.

After cutting out these two pieces, line the peak of the door pattern up with the peak of the cut door to mark the locations for the decorative accents. Drill the holes for a doorknob and doornails and cut the door into sections as indicated on the pattern. Round-over all the edges. Tap the doornails and doorknob (dowels) into place with a hammer and secure with a dab of glue.

## SANDING AND FINISHING

Sand the pieces as needed, then glue and clamp the parts together. After the glue is dry, apply your finish of choice. I apply a dark stain to the sides of the door to add depth and dimension. Apply three coats of polyurethane to the completed door to protect it from the elements.

When the project is complete, attach a sawtooth hanger on the rear of the unit and drive a large-headed nail into the base of your selected tree. Then sit back and wait for word to reach the neighborhood gnomes that they can move right in!

## Tools and Materials

- Sawtooth hanger
- Scroll saw with blades: #9 skip-tooth
- Sanders: palm, tabletop disc (optional)
- Drill press with bits: ¼" (6mm), ½" (13mm) dia.
- Clamps: 7, each 3" (76mm)
- Hammer
- Foam brush
- Pine, 1½" (38mm) thick: arch, 7" x 9" (17.8 x 22.8cm)
- BCX plywood, ¼" (6mm) thick: back, 7" x 9" (17.8 x 22.8cm)
- BCX plywood, ½" (13mm) thick: door, 4¾" x 7¾" (12 x 19.6cm)
- Wood dowel, ¼" (6mm) dia.: 7 each ½" (1.3cm) long
- Wood dowel. ½" (1.3cm) dia.: 1" (2.5cm) long
- Large-headed nail
- Spray adhesive: repositional
- Stain or paint of choice
- Wood glue: waterproof
- Polyurethane: clear gloss
- Sandpaper: assorted
- Rag

## WEATHERING THE DOOR

In order to achieve an aged and weathered appearance, apply a dark stain, such as Minwax® Driftwood, to the front (rough side) of the door piece and allow it to dry. Don't saturate the wood; just streak it on with a thick rag (I use an old sock). After the stain dries, use an electric palm sander with 160-grit sandpaper and sand away most of the stain. Once the polyurethane is applied, the stain remaining in the crevices will give the door a convincing aged look.

Staining the door.

Sanding the door.

# PROJECTS:
# For the Garden

# Lyrical Herb Box

*BY JON DECK*

There's something magical about keeping a garden. Although limited to two raised beds, I manage to cultivate a handful of vegetable varieties each summer. I've never had space to foster an herb garden—but creating a dedicated home for one has always appealed to me.

So, the purpose for this project is evident, as is the inspiration. You don't need to be a child of the sixties to recognize the lyrics to "Scarborough Faire," the lilting ballad by Simon and Garfunkel. Its soft harmonies are as lush the verdant garden I endeavor to keep. And it quite literally speaks to the occupants in the container.

The herb box is freestanding but can be mounted on a wall or beneath a window (see sidebar on page 52). Because the box is designed to live outdoors, the materials used to build it must be weather-resistant or treated to become so. I deliberately painted or sealed all sides of every piece of the box before assembling it.

The basic box is a simple construction, requiring the use of table, jig, and miter saws. The scroll saw is used for the decorative elements—treble clef, music notes, and word art.

## CUTTING THE BOX

All five components of the box can be made from a 24" by 48" (0.6m by 1.2m) craft panel of ¾" (1.9cm) exterior plywood. Using the cutting guide on page 107, cut the box components to the specified dimensions on the table saw.

Using a pencil and a speed square, plot out the legs on the end panels (each foot measures 1" [2.5cm] deep and 1¼" [3.2cm] wide). I added a small radius on the inside corner to soften the look. Cut out the waste on the scroll saw.

Plot out the circles for the plant pots in the top panel. Draw a centerline down the length of the panel. Determine the diameter of the pots that will fit into the box, making sure the pots will not fall through. Do a little math and, using a pencil compass, draw each circle equidistant from the ends and each other. Note: Not all planting pots are round. If necessary, make a cardboard template of your pot's shape to make sure the holes will work. Drill a ⁵⁄₁₆" (8mm)

## Tools and Materials

- Saws: table, jig, miter, scroll saw with #2/0 modified geometry blade
- Nail gun: finish, with 1½" (3.8cm) 16-gauge nails; pin nailer, with ½" (1.2cm) pins
- Measuring tape
- Speed square, pencil/compass
- Drill with bits: ⅛" (3mm), ³⁄₁₆" (4mm), ⁵⁄₁₆" (8mm)-dia.
- Paint roller with 4" (10.2cm) foam roller
- Putty knife
- Hammer (optional)
- Pencil
- Exterior plywood, ¾" (18mm) thick: box, 24" x 48" (0.6 x 1.2m)
- Pine, ¼" (6mm) thick: overlay, 5" x 48" (12.7cm x 1.2m)
- Cedar, ¾" (18mm) thick: box trim, 1½" x 96" (3.8cm x 2.4m)
- Hardboard, ⅛" (3mm) thick: wordart, 6 each 7" x 10" (17.7 x 25.4cm)
- Scrap wood, ⅛" (3mm) thick: spacers, 6 each 1" x 30" (2.5 x 76.2cm)
- Poplar dowel: ³⁄₁₆" (5mm)-dia, 3" (7.6cm) long
- Plant pot: 4 each 6" (15.2cm)-dia.
- Wood glue, water-resistant
- Wood putty
- Tape: blue painter's, packaging
- Spray adhesive
- Sandpaper: 220 grit
- Stain, such as Miniwax® penetrating: dark walnut
- Exterior paint: white
- Spar urethane
- Spray paint: hammered copper

entry hole inside each circle and cut out the holes with the jigsaw.

Then, cut ½" (1.3cm) off the corners of the top panel at 45-degree angles on the miter saw. This will allow water that collects in the top of the box to drain out.

With all the components cut, ease off all the corners and sand the faces and edges of each with 220-grit sandpaper.

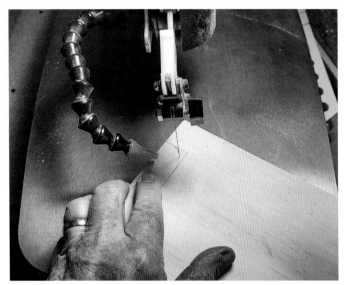

Cut the feet on the end panels.

## PAINTING THE BOX

Stain the front panel on the front face and the top, bottom, and end edges. Allow the stain to dry and apply a clear coat on the stained areas. Let dry.

Paint the reverse side of the front panel, and all surfaces of the other box components with exterior paint. Let dry before assembling.

## ASSEMBLING THE BOX

The box is assembled with a bead of water-resistant wood glue and 1½" (3.8cm) finishing nails on all joints. I used a nail gun and 16-gauge nails, but you can hand nail with a hammer if desired. Start by attaching the

## TIP: BEST SIDE OUT

Exterior plywood is not usually sanded smooth on both sides. Make sure you have the smooth face on the outside of the box when assembling.

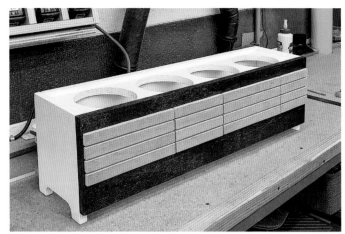

At this point, your box should resemble this.

end panels to the back panel, aligning them at the top of the box.

Apply glue to three edges of the top panel and position in the box assembly recessed ¼" (6mm) from the top. When properly aligned, nail into place. Use a minimum number of nails. The glue will solidly hold the box together, and there will be fewer nail holes to patch later. Set the three-sided box assembly aside.

## MAKING THE OVERLAY

On the table saw, set the fence at ⅞" (2.2cm) and rip four strips at least 36" (0.9m) long from the ¼" (6mm)-thick pine board. Stack the four strips on top of each other and square the end of the stack using the miter saw set at 0 degrees. Then, making sure the ends are aligned, cut the stack at 5" (12.7cm) long, 6" (15.2cm) long, and twice at 9" (22.8cm) long. This will give you 16 slats to build the music staff overlay.

Sand the slats, easing edges and smoothing faces with 220-grit sandpaper. Stain the slats, if desired, and finish them on all sides with a clear coat. When dry, they're ready to mount to the front box panel.

Clamp a strip of scrap wood long enough to span the length of the box panel at 1¼" (3.1cm) from the top edge. Be sure of its position, as it will act as the guide to mounting the slats. Dry-arrange the first row of slats using the Overlay Guide on page 107. Using a ⅛" (3mm)-thick scrap wood strip as a spacer between slats, center the first row on the box panel. Starting on the left, glue down the first slat. Tack the slat in place with the pin nailer. Moving from left to

Stack the music staff slacks before cutting.

right, glue, align with the spacer, and tack fast the first row. Attach subsequent rows using a ⅛" (3mm) spacer between the previous row. When the overlay is complete, attach the front panel to the box assembly.

## ADDING THE TOP TRIM

Cut 45-degree outside corners on the miter saw, making four pieces of the cedar trim to frame the top of the box. Cut two pieces at 28½" (72.4cm) and two at 6¼" (15.9cm) across the inside dimensions of the corners. When cut, arrange them on a flat surface to form a frame. Apply glue to the inside miter cuts and join the pieces, tacking together the outside of the corners with 1½" (38mm) nails. After the glue dries, apply glue to the top edges of the box, position the frame on the box, and then attach with nails. Fill in all the nail holes on the box with wood putty and sand and touch them up with paint or stain as needed. There's no need to patch any of the pin nails.

Use scrap wood for a mounting guide and spacers. Spread glue on the slats to minimize squeeze-out.

Attach the top trim with wood glue and nails.

## MAKING THE NOTES AND WORDART

Stack three pieces of 7" by 10" (17.7cm by 25.4cm) hardboard together with packaging tape, making two stacks. Cover the tops of the stacks with blue painter's tape. Apply the patterns with spray adhesive and cover the patterns with packaging tape. Drill ⅛" (3mm) blade entry holes in all inside frets and on the outside of each pattern line. Resist cutting through to the outside of the stack, as this will weaken the stack as pieces are cut and removed. Cut the interior frets first. When the pieces are cut, carefully sand to remove any fuzzies. Then, spray-paint the pieces, back side first. Be sure to give them a generous coating, but apply multiple coats to avoid runs. Let dry and repeat on the front side of the pieces.

## FINISH THE ASSEMBLY

Lay the box on its back. Dry-position the notes and symbols on the overlay using the Word Art Guide (pages 108-111) for reference. When pleased with the positioning, glue them to the box. Work one at a time. If desired, tack them in place with the pin nailer, but be careful with the narrow stems on the notes. For the dotted notes, drill a ³⁄₁₆" (5mm)-dia., ¼" (6mm)-deep hole in the position shown on the Word Art Guide. Paint both ends of a short length of a ³⁄₁₆" (4mm)-dia. dowel with the same spray paint used for the notes. When dry, cut ⅜" (1cm) off each end to make two dots for the notes. Glue dowels in the holes.

Repeat the same procedure for the word art. Add your plants!

## HANGING THE HERB BOX

The original design of the herb box is freestanding, but it's a snap to modify the project so it can be hung on a garden wall or from a windowsill like a flower box.

Omit the feet on the end panels of the box and make the height the same as the front and back panels (7½" [19cm]). Then, complete the construction of the project as directed in the step text.

To hang the herb box, cut a French cleat* and attach the top half centered on the back panel beneath the cedar trim. You'll have plenty of plywood left over from the board you cut your box components from to make the cleat. Mount the bottom half of the French cleat to the wall and simply hang the box on it. Not only is this method of attachment very solid, but you can easily lift the herb box off the wall whenever you need to attend to your plants.

*Making the cleat is easy. Cut a 7" by 18" (17.7cm by 45.7cm) piece of plywood on the table saw. Then, tilt the blade as close to 45 degrees as you can on your saw. Set the fence for 2" (5cm), and rip the plywood lengthwise. The result is two boards with an angled edge. Mount the narrow board to the box and the wide board to the wall. Gravity will hold your herb box to the wall without using fasteners.

# Plant Markers

*BY JON DECK*

Every gardener knows the anticipation of beholding a garden bursting with colorful produce. However, this sight occurs for a brief time between emergence and harvest. For most of the season, the garden shows only greenery in various stages from shoots to mature plants. These garden markers herald the bounty to come in vibrant fashion.

For most, the backyard garden is a family effort. And this project takes that energy into the workshop. The shapes of the stakes and vegetable cutouts are simple to cut—great for kids and novice scrollers.

Cut the plywood to 8½" by 11" (21.6cm by 27.9cm) panels. I recommend stack cutting to produce multiple stakes and vegetable cutouts. Group the stacks and tightly bind them together on all sides with packaging tape. Cover the face of the stacks with painter's tape and apply the patterns with spray adhesive. Drill blade entry holes and cut out the pieces. Avoid cutting through the edges of the stack.

## Tools and Materials

- Scroll saw with blade: #2 modified geometry
- Drill with ⅛" (3mm)-dia.bit
- Assorted paintbrushes
- Airbrush (optional)
- Woodburner with skew tip (optional)
- Exterior plywood, ¼" (6mm) thick: stakes, 24" (61cm) square
- Plywood, ⅛" (3mm) thick: cutouts, 8½" x 11" (21.6 x 27.9cm)
- Glue: wood, waterproof
- Tape: packaging and painter's
- Spray adhesive
- Primer: flat white latex or gesso
- Art supplies: crayons, markers, paints
- Spar urethane

## MAKING THE PLANT MARKERS

When they're cut, everyone can color the veggies. The patterns are colored as suggestions, but anything goes. Decorate the cutouts with crayons, markers, and paints with brushes or an airbrush. Just be sure to coat both sides with weather-resistant clear varnish to protect your finished artwork.

Glue the colored cutouts onto the basic stakes with a waterproof wood glue. Center the cutout, or glue it a little higher if you prefer to label the stake with the name of the plant. A woodburner with a skew tip works well here.

## BRIGHT COLORS

Coat the cutouts with flat white primer or gesso to ensure the pigments applied don't lose their brilliance.

**You can also paint the basic stakes, stain them, or leave them natural. Don't forget to varnish both the stakes and cutouts.**

# Plant Markers Patterns

Photocopy at 100%

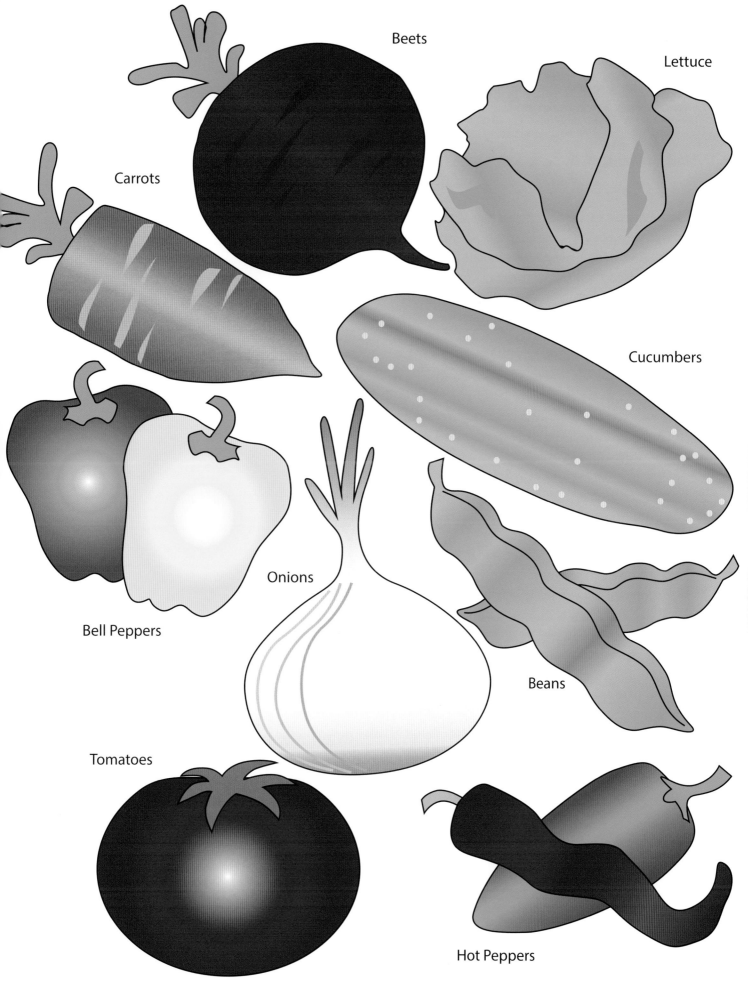

Beets

Lettuce

Carrots

Cucumbers

Bell Peppers

Onions

Beans

Tomatoes

Hot Peppers

# Potato Planter

**Tools and Materials**
- Tape measure
- Drill with bits: assorted
- Saws: reciprocating, jig saw, or circular
- Angle grinder
- Sander: orbital (optional)
- Wooden shipping pallets
- Decking screws, 1½" (3.2cm) long

I had never tried growing potatoes, but when I heard about the potato box concept, I was intrigued. Some of the sources I found claim more than 100 pounds (45kg) of potatoes can be grown in a compact 2' by 2' (6.1 by 6.1m) area, making this method one of the most efficient gardening setups available. A rule of thumb is that 1 pound (.5kg) of seed potatoes can yield 100 pounds (45kg) of potatoes at harvest time. If you're trying to produce even more than that, this concept will scale quite easily: a 4', 6', or even 8' (1.2, 1.8, or 2.4m) potato bin could be built to multiply the bounty.

The technique essentially grows potatoes vertically, but not through the use of trellises, as is the case with many other plants. Instead, you simply build a box around a cluster of potato plants and, as they grow, cover them with mulch and straw. This forces the plants to grow ever higher, and they'll continue to set potatoes in the "underground" portion below the exposed foliage. Make sure to keep some of the leaves exposed—they do need to conduct photosynthesis, after all.

This potato box features modular sides that are screwed on as the plants grow taller, thus providing more space for your potato crop to develop. The slats don't have to be snug to each other, as the box itself can be filled in with straw and mulch. The main roots of the plants are established deep in the ground, so the material used to fill in the bin as the plants grow functions more as a cover for the plants than as a nutritional medium. The ground below the planter, however, needs to be prepared, as that is the soil where the plants will establish themselves and draw nutrients.

Later in the season, you can remove the sides lower down on the box and steal some potatoes while the plants continue to grow, or you can just remove the screws and easily dig through the filler. This method has the advantage of not requiring you to thrust a pitchfork into the ground, which can damage potatoes.

While you can use ordinary potatoes from the grocery store that have begun to sprout, I recommend planting seed potatoes that are known to be disease-free. Any good garden store should have them; I paid less than $1.50 for a whole bunch. And since I used a couple of free shipping pallets to build the box, this project was among the most economical that I've ever built, too.

**1. Gather your materials.** The humble pallet has many things to offer to a resourceful DIYer. Its main advantage is probably its price: I don't mind having to do a little work to strip away the useful lumber when it costs nothing.

**2. Prepare the wood.** Focus on the center sections which have fewer nails. Use a reciprocating saw, jigsaw, or circular saw to quickly remove the nail-infested end portions of the pallet. This method leaves a number of fairly long (almost 36" [91.4cm]) strips of lumber from the center of the pallet.

**3. Free the boards.** To separate the strips from the center support, don't try to pull the nails. It is faster to remove the strips by twisting them. Then remove any sharp nail pieces. An angle grinder quickly cuts away any nails that remain and a reciprocating saw does a great job of powering through stubborn fasteners.

**4. Attach the first slat.** Select four pieces of 2x2 lumber from the pallet's thicker support pieces and use them as vertical corner posts. Screw the first strips to the posts. Placing the elements on a stable assembly surface helps to ensure proper alignment between the parts. This will become important later when you try to add the extra side pieces—if the frame is out of square, the boards won't fit!

**5. Build two sides.** I used two strips at the bottom to keep the assembly rigid, and one at the top to keep the posts from splaying out irregularly. Use a tape measure to verify that the diagonal measurements are equal—this indicates that the side panel is square.

**6. Assemble the frame.** Attach a couple of strips to one of the side panels and finish by screwing the other side in place. The completed potato box is lightweight and easy to move around, so you don't have to build it on site if that isn't convenient.

**7**

**7. Set up the planter.** Take the planter frame where you want to grow your potatoes. Make sure that the placement of the bin allows access to all sides—don't push ours up against the fence to save space in the yard. You'll need enough room to screw the extra side pieces on as the potatoes grow. Dig up the soil a bit so you can set the frame relatively flat on the ground. Plant the seed potatoes. My young daughter, Abigail, is already an avid gardener, and she couldn't resist hopping inside and doing some digging.

## POTATO RATIO

1 pound (.5kg) of seed potatoes can yield 100 pounds (45kg) of potatoes at harvest time.

| | Part | Qty. | Materials | Dimensions |
|---|---|---|---|---|
| **POTATO PLANTER PARTS LIST** | | | | |
| A | Posts | 4 | 2" (5.1cm) square | 48" (1.2m) |
| B | Side strips | 32 | ⅝" (1.6cm) thick: 3½" to 4½" (9 to 11.4cm) wide boards | 36" (0.9m) |
| C | Screws | As needed | Exterior-grade decking screws | 1½" (5.1cm) long |

The completed planter box.

## FINISHING

Add slats as needed. A few weeks in, the plants will be well established and growing like crazy. After six weeks, I had added a number of tiers to the box so it was almost waist-height. When the plants grow above the current highest slat, screw on the next level and fill up to that point with straw or mulch. Be sure to keep some leaves showing!

## POTATO VARIETIES

There are countless varieties of potatoes, and each variety should be planted at a specific time of year. Here are a few varieties you might want to include in your garden:

| POTATO VARIETIES | | | |
|---|---|---|---|
| Name | Planting Time | Days to Maturity | Notes |
| AC Peregrine Red | Late season | 100–120 days | Lasts a long time in storage |
| Caribe | Mid-season | 55–70 days | Excellent baked |
| Goldrush | Late season | 100–120 days | Good baked, mashed, in stews, or for perogi |
| Norland | Early season | 70–85 days | Bright red skin |
| Red Pontiac | Late season | 100–120 days | Drought-tolerant variety |
| Viking | Mid-season | 85–100 days | Popular gardening variety |
| Yukon Gold | Mid-season | 85–100 days | Great for perogi |

# Cold Frame

*BY NICK HAMILTON*

Cold frames are relatively easy to make, and this is a far cheaper option than buying a similar-quality product. All that is required to make one is rough-sawn lumber and a few tools.

## Tools and Materials

- Boards: support posts, 2" (5cm) square, 60" (1.5m) long
- Boards: front, back, sides, 1 ¾" x 4" (4.4 x 10.1cm), 32' (9.7m) long
- Boards: front and back of lid, 2 each 1" x 1¾" (2.5 x 4.4cm), 4' (1.2m) long
- Boards: end and central lid supports, 3 each 1" x 1 ¾" (2.5 x 4.4cm), 21" (53cm) long
- Metal angle brackets: 8 each 3"-long (7.6cm)
- Hinges: 3 each 2" (5cm) long
- Metal latch
- Wood screws: ¾" (2cm), 2 ¾" (7cm)
- Wooden batten: ½" (13mm) thick, 13 ¾' (3.6m) long
- Plastic sheeting
- Nails: 2" (5cm)
- Wood preservative: organic

**5**

| COLD FRAME CUT LIST | | |
|---|---|---|
| Item | Qty. | Dimensions |
| Front support posts | 2 | 12" x 2" square (30 x 5cm square) |
| Rear support posts | 2 | 16" x 2" square (40 x 5cm square) |
| Front and back | 7 | 4' x 1¾" x 4" (120 x 4cm x 10cm) |
| Two sides | 8 | 21" x 1¾" x 4" (52.5 x 4cm x 10cm) |
| Front and back of lid | 2 | 4' x 1" x 1¾" (1.2m x 2.5cm x 4cm) |
| End and central support of lid | 3 | 21" x 1" x 1¾" (53 x 2.5 x 4cm) |

**The first job is to cut virtually all the wood into these lengths.**

**1. Prepare the two side pieces.** Cut down the lengths of two side pieces of wood so that 1" (2½cm) is removed from the length of each. The six lengths of wood that make up the main part of each side (three per side) are screwed to the supporting posts first, so that all wood is flush, ensuring that one of the cut-down pieces is on each side. Do not worry about the excess supporting post at the rear of the cold frame.

**2. Attach the front and backs.** Attach both the front and back lengths of wood so that they overlap the ends of the sides already in place. This will leave a box with gaps on the supporting posts on each side, but two spare 21" (52.5cm) lengths of 4" x 1¾" (10 x 4cm). Each of these can be held up to the gaps on the sides and the sloping cut from the back of the cold frame down to the front marked for sawing. Once sawn, screw in place. Using a saw, angle the tops of the rear posts so all the pieces of wood are flush. This forms the base of the cold frame, except for handles that will be used to move it.

**3. Make the handles.** Either cut hand-sized holes into each end if a jigsaw is handy, or attach small extra pieces from the 1¾" x 1" (4 x 2.5cm) wood. The latter is done by screwing two vertical pieces into the sides; a horizontal piece of wood is then screwed in place to bridge the gap.

**4. Make the lid.** Attach the two 4' (120cm) lengths of 1¾" x 1" (4 x 2.5cm) wood and two of the 21" (53cm) lengths of 1¾" x 1" (4 x 2.5cm) wood together using four of the metal angle brackets. The lid needs to be exactly the same size as the top of the cold-frame base. Attach the last 21" (53cm) length of 1¾" x 1" (4 x 2.5cm) wood to the center of the lid using the remaining four brackets. Before going any further, treat the basic framework of the cold frame with an organic wood preservative.

**5. Attach the lid.** Screw the hinges into place, with one hinge in the center of the back of the lid and the other two each 6" (15cm) in from each end. Attach plastic sheeting to the top of the lid, place it over the lid with about 3" (8cm) overhanging all around. Cut the wood piece into four pieces to correspond to the four sides of the box. Roll the plastic around each 1" x 2" (2.5 x 5cm) wooden piece and nail onto the lid close to the outer edge, ensuring it is tight with no creases in it. I like to use plastic instead of glass or plexiglass because these two materials are easy to crack or break, particularly on windy days. Close the lid and screw the latch into place in the center of the lid and base.

# Rainwater Harvester

*BY CHRIS GLEASON*

My family lives in a dry area—Salt Lake City, Utah, to be precise—and people in this region frequently worry about the threat of drought. Most of our municipal water comes from snow melt in the nearby mountains, and while we've been fortunate to have seen some pretty big snowfalls in recent years, a bad year could pose real problems for the million-plus people who call the area home.

Note: *Rainwater harvest systems like this are ideal for watering gardens, but they are not to be used for drinking water. This simple rain barrel doesn't offer any means to purify the water to the level required for direct human consumption.*

## Tools and Materials

- Clamps
- Band saw
- Scroll saw
- Power drill with twist drill bits
- Garden hose
- Garden hose valve: threaded with neoprene washer
- Flexible connector
- Tape measure
- Barrel: 55 gallon (208 liter)
- Plywood: ¾" (1.9cm) thick, various sizes
- Plywood: ⅛" (3mm) thick for roof
- Screws: various sizes
- Hinges: concealed
- Paint: optional for exterior
- Wire filter

## TIP: GETTING HELP

Many locales offer incentives for rainwater collection, including free storage barrels. Check with your water company.

| | Part | Quantity | Materials | Dimensions |
|---|---|---|---|---|
| | **RAINWATER HARVESTER PARTS LIST** | | | |
| A | Legs | 4 | 2x2 (61 x 61cm) | 62" (157.5cm) |
| B | Side panels | 2 | ⅜" (1cm) plywood | 45" x 32" (114.3 x 815mm) |
| C | Back panel | 1 | ⅜" (1cm) plywood | 45" x 32" (114.3 x 815mm) |
| D | Floor cleats | 2 | 2x4 (61 x 121.9cm) | 32" (81.3cm) |
| E | Floor panel | 1 | ¾" (1.9cm) plywood | 30" x 29" (76 x 73.7cm) |
| F | Top rail | 2 | ¾" (1.9cm) plywood | 32" x 6" (815 x 150mm) |
| G | Door panel | 1 | ⅜" (1cm) plywood | 45" x 32" (114.3 x 815mm) |
| H | Door stiles | 2 | 1x3 (30.5 x 91.4cm) | 44" (111.8cm) |
| I | Door bottom rail | 1 | 1x3 (30.5 x 91.4cm) | 25" (63.5cm) |
| J | Door top rail | 1 | 1x6 (30.5 x 182.9cm) | 25" (63.5cm) |
| K | Door handle | 1 | | |
| L | Door hinges | 1 pair | | |
| M | Roof | 1 | ⅛" (3mm) plywood | 40" x 36" (101.7cm x 915mm) |
| N | Roof supports | 2 | ¾" (1.9cm)-thick plywood | 32" x 7" (81.3 x 17.8cm) |
| O | 55-gallon (208-liter) barrel with lid | 1 | | |
| P | Downspout fittings | As needed | | |
| Q | Hose bib | 1 | | |
| R | Neoprene washer | 1 | | |
| S | Threaded valve | 1 | | |
| T | Filter | 1 | | |

## WORDS ON WATER USE

As I researched, I got interested in the way my family and I use water in and around our home, and I learned a lot. For one thing, we use a lot of water! To determine how much water you use every year, I highly recommend checking out an online water-use calculator. The basic calculations will only take a few minutes, and it will provide a frame of reference for discussing using water in your garden.

Collecting water from a small shed roof, as this system does, provides 25%–30% of the water that we need annually for our garden. So, from that perspective, it is something to feel good about.

## HOW MUCH RAINFALL CAN YOU COLLECT?

To determine the amount of water that you could potentially collect during the year, just follow these steps.

1. First, figure out the square footage of the roof. You want the width multiplied by the length.

2. Convert the square footage into square inches by multiplying by 144.

3. Multiply the square inch measurement of your roof by the average annual inches of rainfall for your area. This number is how many cubic inches of rain will fall on your roof in a year.

4. Finally, convert the cubic inches into gallons by dividing the number by 231 (that's how many cubic inches are in a gallon).

## EFFICIENCY

No rainwater collection system is 100% efficient, as evaporation, run-off, and leaks will have some effect. Most estimates state that you can plan on capturing 70%–90% of the amount of rain that falls. So, in this case, harvesting 80% of the rainfall would yield 837 gallons per year. That would seem to indicate a need for several 55-gallon (208-liter) barrels to ensure that I'm able to collect all of the available rainfall. But, in reality, less capacity is probably just fine, since the rainfall and usage are both spread across the whole year. As rain comes down, I'm really only storing it for a fairly short time before using it, so I don't need a year's worth of capacity.

With this in mind, I have a couple of options. A single (55 gallon) barrel system would probably be adequate, since I planned on using the water pretty frequently, and rainstorms are not particularly common in this area. Not sure how much rain your area receives in a year? I wasn't either, but the information is just a quick internet search away.

How much water will your garden need over the course of a season? As a general guideline, you can figure that watering with sprinklers (or a hose), one time per week in the amount of 1" to 2" (2.5 to 5.1cm) of moisture will require 65–130 gallons (246–492 liters) per 100 square feet (9.3 square meters). Note that drip irrigation will generally provide a more efficient use of water, as less is lost to evaporation, and the water is targeted directly to the plants that you're trying to cultivate.

## CHOOSING A TYPE OF SYSTEM

The type of rainwater harvesting system that you decide to build will depend, like most things, on what you're trying to accomplish and what you are willing to spend. To get the most that Mother Nature has to offer, you'll want to maximize both your collection and storage. If you live in a wet area, such as the Pacific Northwest, you may be able to harvest enough rain to meet your household's needs for 8–10 months out of the year for as little as just a couple of thousand dollars. At the other end of the spectrum, a single barrel system will help provide a good portion of the water that your garden will need, at a cost of $50–$100. Where do you hope to land on this continuum? I recommend doing some more in-depth research to help you decide, but I hope this discussion can provide some food for thought to get you started.

## GRAVITY SYSTEM

The simplest type of system utilizes gravity to do all the work. Gutters collect rainwater and channel it into a barrel, and a hose at the bottom of the barrel can be moved around to draw on the water supply as needed. If you position the barrel up on a stand in a location where the barrel is higher than the beds you plan to water, this is probably all the water pressure you'll need. Remember that the higher the water, the more water pressure will be generated. You cannot just stick a hose in a barrel, start a siphon, and expect it to keep flowing—unless the water source is higher than where you are directing the end of the hose.

## DRIP IRRIGATION SYSTEM

Even though rain barrels are pretty simple, they do offer a choice in watering methods: you can simply water with a hose, or, by adding on inexpensive kits available online, you can use barrels for drip irrigation. Drip irrigation kits are important if you plan to use rain barrels without a pump, because most drip systems require much higher pressure than a gravity-fed system can generate. To compensate for this, several manufacturers have created kits that still allow you to enjoy the efficiency of drip irrigation without the need for an electric pump.

**2. Measure the barrel.** I began the actual construction by measuring our barrel—a standard 55-gallon (208-liter) barrel (O) we obtained for free from a local brewery. This determined the size of the enclosure required.

**3. Attach the side panels to the legs.** The enclosure I built was super simple, but it is very sturdy, and it has held up quite well. It consists of two identical plywood side panels (B) that are each screwed to a pair of 2" (5.1cm) square legs (A).

**1. Choose a spot.** The most logical layout should be pretty intuitive: since you'll be harvesting the rainwater that falls onto a roof, you'll want to identify the roof pitch that is in the best spot, and where a barrel might be placed. Unless you are interested in building a more complex system with an electric pump, the barrel will need to be situated above the area that you'll be watering—this factor alone may make your decision for you. For us, we had an out-of-control rose bush that looked nice, but wasn't providing anything edible, so we decided to clear it out and put in a rain barrel and raised bed. The hardest part was getting around to it. Once I got going, it only took about half an hour to prep the site.

**4**

**5**

**6**

**4. Attach the two side assemblies.** I connected the two side panel assemblies to each other by running a back panel (C) between them and fastening it into place with screws. I did the work with the whole assembly laid down on the floor because it was easier to work with gravity rather than fight against it.

**5. Install floor cleats.** The enclosure needed a very strong floor because a full barrel is heavy—over 400 pounds (181kg). To support the floor panel, I attached a set of 2x4 (3.8 x 8.9cm) cleats (D) to the sides (B) and to the legs (A) with screws. A clamp held them in place temporarily.

**6. Install the floor.** The floor panel (E) itself was made of ¾" (18mm) plywood. I screwed it securely into the cleats (D). If you're after a really Spartan look, you could probably just stop here. This ultra-simple assembly would probably work fine, although you might want to reinforce the top of the structure to keep the whole thing from wobbling. The roof actually helps to make it a lot more rigid.

**7**

**7. Assemble the door.** This door was built very simply from a ⅜" (10mm) plywood panel (G) and dressed up with a frame (H–J) made from 1x3s that I screwed directly to the front of the panel. Dress up the door however you want. I cut the top rail in an arch shape for decorative purposes.

**8. Attach the hinges.** This door was attached with simple concealed hinges (L) because I had them laying around. Use whatever works for you.

**9. Establish the roof curve.** The unique curved roof of the enclosure is made from ⅛" (3mm) plywood (M) on a scroll saw and held in place on the ends by a pair of corresponding ¾" (19mm)-thick plywood supports (N). To determine the shape of the roof, I bent the panel into an eye-pleasing curve and tacked the corners with screws.

**10. Mark the roof curve.** To scribe the profile onto the supports (N), I simply held them up and traced the shape of the curve onto the back of the supports. I used a band saw to cut them to size.

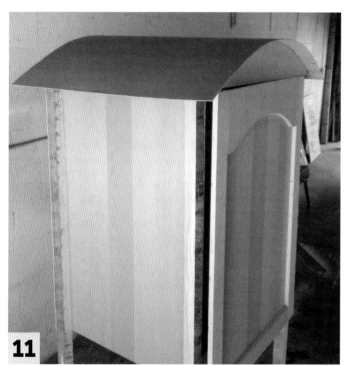

**11. Attach the roof.** The completed supports (N) were then screwed to the stilts (A). With the supports in place, it was pretty easy to put the roof (M) back on and run screws through the roof panel and into the edge of the supports. The result was really sturdy, and it helped keep the whole thing light enough to move around with ease. The curved shape allowed me to create a very strong roof that shed snow very readily, even though the material itself was surprisingly thin. Paint the exterior, if desired.

**12. Hook up the system.** Plumbing the barrel is really simple— you just need to add an extension (P) to the gutters so that water drains into the barrel (O). This will probably require a flexible connector, depending on where exactly your barrel is positioned.

**13**

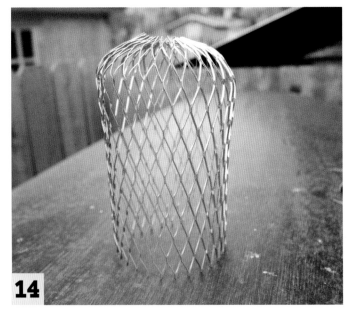

**14**

**13. Install the threaded valve.** The water will drain from the barrel (O) via a simple threaded valve (S) that will attach to a standard garden hose. If your barrel has a hole in it at the bottom, size the valve to fit that. If not, use a twist drill bit on a power drill to create a hole. Make sure you put scrap wood behind where you're drilling to keep the drilling steady. Make sure to install the valve with a neoprene washer (R) to keep water from leaking around the hole.

**14. Install a filter.** A filter (T) is required somewhere along the line to keep large chunks of debris out of the water. I used a wire filter that goes right on top of the drain hole in the gutter.

## BONUS: GROWING GREAT TOMATOES

1. **Location:** Tomatoes like early morning sun and require good air circulation; plan for 1' (30.5cm) of space around each full-grown plant. Prevent the spread of disease by staggering your tomatoes throughout your garden rather than planting them right next to each other.

2. **Planting tricks:** Dig a large hole, mix compost with the soil, and refill the hole until just a few inches of the tomato seedling will be above ground. Remove any leaves that would be underground, put the seedling in the hole, and loosely fill the soil and compost mixture around the plant.

3. **The secret ingredient:** Prevent blossom-end rot by adding about a dozen dry, finely crushed eggshells to each planting hole before placing in the seedlings.

4. **Supporting the plants:** Tomatoes are vines, and heirloom varieties can grow up to 14' (4.3m) long and bear clusters of fruit weighing more than 10lbs (4.5kg). Instead of trying to tie the huge and heavy vine to a stake or support it with a small store-bought cage, make your own cages using sturdy wire fencing (not chicken wire). Cut 5' (1.5m)-tall fencing into

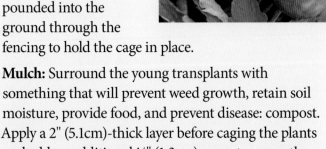

6' (1.8m) lengths, bend the spokes from one side around the other to secure it in a circle, and use long stakes pounded into the ground through the fencing to hold the cage in place.

5. **Mulch:** Surround the young transplants with something that will prevent weed growth, retain soil moisture, provide food, and prevent disease: compost. Apply a 2" (5.1cm)-thick layer before caging the plants and add an additional ½" (1.3cm) every two months during the growing season. Avoid wood mulch, as it can cultivate disease.

6. **Water:** Never water tomatoes in the evening. In fact, if your garden gets one soaking storm a week, you will rarely need to water them at all. Tomatoes need about 1" (2.5cm) of water per week, preferably delivered all at once, slowly, to the roots, in the early morning. Let the plants dry out completely between waterings.

# PROJECTS:
# Furniture & Larger Builds

# Hammock Stand

*BY BILL HYLTON*

**Tools and Materials**

- Palm planer
- Belt sander
- Clamps
- Drill with bits: assorted
- Tape measure
- Speed square
- Paintbrush (optional)
- Pine, various thicknesses: see Parts List
- Glue: wood, stick
- Screws: 2" (5.1cm) and 3" (7.6cm) decking
- Screw eyes: double-sided
- Repair links: 2 each 5⁄16" x 3" (8mm x 7.6cm)
- Finish, such as water-resistant solid-color stain (optional)
- 7¼" (18.4cm) circular saw, or table saw and miter saw

There's nothing like a spacious, comfortable hammock for relaxing outside on a summer day. But there's always a hitch. You have the perfect spot for the hammock, but can't seem to figure out how to support it. Generally, you need to hang the hammock from hooks set 12'–5' feet apart, and 4'–5' feet off the ground. Set the supports too close together or too far apart, and you'll sag into the hammock, or flip right out of it. You also need to find support trees or posts that are pretty stout.

A hammock stand is often a better solution. You can make the proportions just right for comfort and move the assembly wherever you want it. Once the frame is built, you can screw in your hooks just the right distance apart and just the right height off the ground. The sturdy main struts on this stand have enough capacity to handle just about any hammock on the market. If that perfect site in your backyard gets too sunny, the solution is simple: just move your new hammock stand to a better location.

| HAMMOCK STAND PARTS LIST | | | | |
|---|---|---|---|---|
| | Part | Quantity | Materials | Dimensions |
| A | Stretcher | 2 | PT Lumber, 2x4 | 1½" x 3½" x 168" (3.8cm x 8.9cm x 4.3m) |
| B | Spine | 1 | PT Lumber, 2x4 | 1½" x 3½" x 62" (3.8cm x 8.9cm x 1.6m) |
| C | Cross member | 2 | PT Lumber, 4x4 | 3½" x 3½" x 60" (8.9cm x 8.9cm x 1.5m) |
| D | Strut | 2 | PT Lumber, 2x4 | 1½" x 3½" x 78" (3.8cm x 8.9cm x 2m) |
| E | Post | 2 | PT Lumber, 2x4 | 1½" x 3½" x 36½" (3.8cm x 8.9cm x 92.7cm) |
| F | Long strut facing | 4 | PT Lumber, 5 /4x6 (ripped) | 1" x 2¾" x 48⁹⁄16" (2.5cm x 7cm x 1.2m) |
| G | Short strut facing | 4 | PT Lumber, 5 /4x6 (ripped) | 1" x 2¾" x 22¼" (2.5cm x 7cm x 56.5cm) |
| H | Post facing | 4 | PT Lumber, 5 /4x6 (ripped) | 1" x 2¾" x 37⅛" (2.5 x 7 x 94.3cm) |

## MATERIALS

You may be able to pull your hammock stand under a porch roof. But it's wise to choose materials that will stand up to the elements. Over the winter, you could partially dismantle the stand by turning out the screws from the cross members and storing the major sections in the garage or shed.

To withstand the exposure, the best plan is to use pressure-treated (PT) wood. It is strong and durable, and widely available in the stock sizes you need for this project. You can dress up the finished piece with stain.

Special precautions are needed when working with PT wood, as the sawdust is infused with harmful chemicals. While manufacturers insist that PT wood is safe, it's wise to wear a dust mask and eye protection when cutting it. Also, sweep up the sawdust, and make sure the debris gets carted away with the trash (where

## BUILDER'S NOTES

The hammock stand is a simple project that even a novice woodworker can tackle with success. But it's a good idea to build the stand outside because it's a long and cumbersome piece of furniture that may be too big to work on conveniently in a home shop.

I supported the assembly on a pair of sawhorses and used an extra 16-foot 2x4 to help support the upper ends of the posts and struts during the assembly process.

permitted by local ordinances). Don't burn scraps of PT wood in your fireplace or woodstove.

## TOOLS AND TECHNIQUES

You need two power tools to build the stand: a circular saw to crosscut and miter the frame parts and to make the facings and a drill-driver to fasten the parts together.

A 7¼" (184mm) circular saw will handle all the 90- and 45-degree crosscuts. (Use a square to guide your circular saw as you make the cuts.) You also can use the circular saw with a guide to rip the 5/4 stock. If you have access to a table saw for the rips and a power miter saw to handle the crosscuts and miters, the cutting will be easier and faster.

## FINISH

I used a water-repellent solid-color stain on the hammock stand—just to conceal the green tinge of the wood. The water-based stain spreads smoothly and makes it easy to clean up the brush with soap and water.

## MEASURING

Determine how far apart the suspension hooks need to be set for the hammock. There's no point in making the stand larger than necessary.

Typically, a new hammock will include printed instructions (and warnings) that indicate a range of measurements for properly positioning the suspension points. The printed material with the hammock I bought indicated the suspension points should be 13' to 15' (4 to 4.6m) apart and 4' to 5' (1.2 to 1.5m) above the ground. This stand is designed around those guidelines, with the final suspension points just 13' (4m) apart and 4½ (1.4m) feet above the ground.

Altering the stand's dimensions to accommodate your hammock is not difficult. Examine the side elevation drawing, noting the distance between the hangers and between the ground and each hanger. To increase the distance between hangers, increase the length of the stretchers and spine, and then move the posts and struts out.

Stretch out your hammock on the ground, and measure it from end to end before you start construction. Those dimensions will determine roughly how far apart the suspension points must be on your stand.

## MAKING CROSS MEMBERS

Begin by cutting the 4x4 cross members, shaping the ends and cutting the laps for the stretchers. I cut both cross members from a 10-foot-long 4x4. You can make overall cuts while squaring up the ends, if necessary, and then simply cut the post in two.

Because the girth of the cross members exceeds the cutting capacity of the typical circular saw, you need to cut the 4x4 in two passes. Normally, you make these cuts using the full depth of the blade. That way, cuts from opposite sides of the piece will meet up. You will need to follow your square lines very carefully to get the two cuts level.

Lay out and cut the tapered ends. Follow the layout shown in the drawing, and then mark out cut lines on both sides of the cross member, connecting them with lines across the ends and the top surface. Make the cuts in the same way you cut the cross members. Cut a little more than halfway through the stock from one face, and then roll the piece over and make a second cut. Use a power planer or belt sander to smooth the sawn surface.

The laps are located equidistant from the ends of each 5' (1.5m)-long cross member, and are cut into the top surface. Following the drawing again, mark the laps on the cross members. The depth of the laps is 1¾" (4.5cm), which is half the stock width. The width of the laps is 4½" (11.4cm), which is the thickness of three 2x4s stacked face-to-face.

Cut the laps using your circular saw. Adjust the cutting depth to the layout line on one of the cross members. The two critical cuts on each lap are the shoulder cuts. Guide the saw with a square as you cut them so that you produce crisp, square cuts. The stretcher-and-spine assembly needs to fit tightly between the shoulders. Having cut the shoulders, set the square aside, and make repeated, closely spaced cuts to remove the material between them.

## MAKING STRETCHERS

Shape the ends of the stretchers and cut the laps in them for the cross members. The 2x4 stretchers are 14 feet long. Select two straight 2x4s, trim them to equal lengths, and, in the process, square the ends. *Note: You should be able to make these cuts without altering the cut-depth setting on your circular saw.* You want to cut laps in the stretchers at the same setting used to lap the cross members. Lay out the tapers on the ends, and then saw to the cut lines with your circular saw. Clean up the freshly cut tapered edges with the power planer or the belt sander.

Cut the laps for the bottom edges of the stretchers. The depth of the laps is 1¾" (4.5cm), which is half the stock width. The width of the laps is 3½" (89mm), which is the width of the 4x4 cross members. Clamp

Cut the lap pockets for the stretchers and cross members with a circular saw. Clamp the stretchers together, and make repeated, closely-spaced passes to clear the pocket. Clean up the edges with a planer or sander.

the two stretchers together, and lay out the laps as shown in the drawings on page 113.

Cut the laps with your circular saw. As before, the critical cuts are the shoulder cuts. Once you make them, continue with repeated, closely spaced cuts to the waste material between them.

Use a guide with your circular saw to make true cuts for the spine, posts, and struts. This speed square can be adjusted to any angle between 45° and 90°, and is useful on the many miter cuts.

## CUTTING MAJOR SUPPORTS

The spine and the posts are the only parts you need to cut to a specific length at this time. Cut the spine to the length specified on the Parts List (see page 70). Miter both ends at 45 degrees. Cut each of the two posts for the stand from a different 10-foot 2x4. Lay out each post and make the miters. The remaining length of stock, with one end miter-cut at 45 degrees, is the strut. You will need to trim each strut to final length late in the assembly process, but for now, each strut is a piece roughly 7' (2.1m) long.

## BASIC ASSEMBLY

Screw the spine, posts, and struts to one of the stretchers, beginning with the spine. Mark the centerpoint on both the stretcher and the spine, lay one piece on the other, align the marks, and flush-up the edges. Then drive three or four 2" (51mm) deck screws through the spine into the stretcher.

Next, position one of the struts. It should angle off the stretcher at 45 degrees. One edge should be tight against the end of the spine, and the mitered end

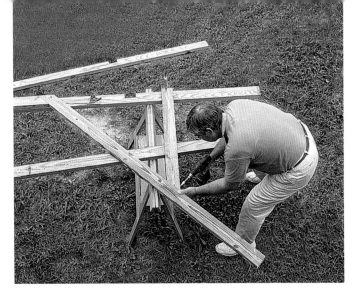

Set the stretcher across sawhorses along with an extra 2x4 to support the free ends of the posts and struts and keep them level. Here, I'm driving a screw through the post into the strut.

At this point, you can right the stand and complete the assembly, or you can leave it on its side across the sawhorses while you fit and attach the facings.

Settle the cross members and stretchers into the lap joints, and secure with 3" (76mm) screws driven through the bottom of each cross member. Use a clamp to squeeze the stretchers together.

should be flush with the bottom edge of the stretcher. To make things easier, support the free end of the strut on an extra 2x4 laid on the sawhorses, parallel with the stretcher. To fasten the assembly, drive several 2" (51mm) screws through the strut into the stretcher.

Work on the post next. Don't be too concerned about positioning it at this stage. Align the post so that the mitered end is tight against the underside of the strut and the square end is flush with the bottom edge of the stretcher. When the post is perpendicular to the stretcher, drive in several 2" (51mm) screws. Also drive a 3" (76mm)-long deck screw through the post edge into the strut. Use this approach to install the other strut and post at the other end of the assembly.

Then set the second stretcher in place and screw it down, using 3" (76mm)-long screws. Drive four screws through the stretcher into each post and strut, and then drive several screws through the stretcher into the spine. Carefully roll the assembly over and drive 3" (76mm) screws through the top stretcher into the assembly.

## CROSS MEMBERS

You've already cut the laps in the stretchers and the cross members, but this is the first opportunity to fit the parts together. Ideally, it will take only modest persuasion to close the joints. Seat the cross members; then drive 3" (76mm) screws through the 4x4s into the stretchers.

## FACINGS

The facings are strips of 5/4 stock screwed to the faces of the struts and posts. The critical pieces are the ones that face the posts because they overlap the butt joint between the post and strut and lock the pieces together. To create a little visual interest, I ripped the facing strips to a 3" (7.6cm) width, leaving a ¼" (6mm) reveal between the edges of the struts and posts and their facings. This looks better than leaving the edges flush.

The first job is to rip the stock to width. Pressure-treated 5/4 is typically stocked in the form of 5/4x6 decking. It is 5½" (14cm) wide, with radiused edges. To use the material as facing in this project, rip off the radiused edges, which will reduce the width to 3" (7.6cm). Rip down the four 10-footers to make the facings using a table saw or a circular saw with a sturdy rip guide. It's best to first crosscut each 10-footer into three pieces: a 52" (132cm)-long piece, a 40" (101cm)-long piece, and a 28" (71cm)-long piece andf then rip them.

The individual facings should be cut to fit. To begin, miter one end of a 52" (132cm) at 45°. Set the 40" (101cm) on the post, and line it up with the ¼" (6mm) reveal along the edges. Set the 52" (132cm) on the strut with the miter against the stretcher and the square end overlapping the post-facing. Line it up, and mark it (and

Fit the facings by centering the rough-length facing and the strut facing on the post. Mark and scribe the edges of the strut facing where it overlaps the post facing, and then miter the two pieces.

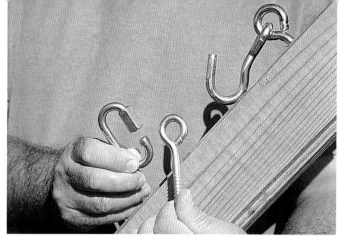

Use a stout screw eye with a 3" (76mm) shank, and use a beefy repair link to connect the hammock to the screw eye. The hammock I bought included screw eyes and hooks. You may need to buy hardware.

the post facing) for trimming where they meet. Miter the ends of these pieces, and screw them to the post and strut. Ultimately, you will drive several 3" (76mm) screws through the upper end of the post facing into the post and strut. But don't do it until a facing piece has been applied to both sides of these parts.

Lastly, cut and install the four post facings and long-strut facings.

Wait to apply the short-strut facings until you've installed the suspension hardware and trimmed the strut.

## HARDWARE

Before cutting and attaching the last four pieces of facing, you need to trim the struts. Before you do that, you need to find where you must locate the hardware.

Attach the mitered facings to the frame with screws. Lock the post and strut together with 3" (76mm) screws. They will penetrate the facing and frame and extend into the facing on the opposite side.

For my hammock, the hooks needed to be 13' (3.9m) apart and at least 4' (1.2m) above the ground. To start, I measured and marked the spot on each strut that was just 4' (1.2m) vertically from the ground. Then, I measured horizontally from point to point of my vertical marks and found them to be less than the required 13' (3.9m) apart. To meet the required horizontal measurement, I simply slid the attachment points toward the ends of the struts. (This is one place where it pays to measure carefully, and more than once.)

The attachment hardware I used was supplied with the hammock. If that's not the case for you, use a pair of screw eyes and repair links. With the points located and marked, simply drill pilot holes to avoid splitting, and turn the screw eye into the struts.

Next, mark and trim the struts. I crosscut the struts 3½" (8.9cm) from the screw eye. With the struts trimmed, you can lay out and cut the remaining pieces of facing and attach them. Now the hammock stand is ready for finishing.

## FINISHING

If you use pressure-treated wood, you don't really need a finish. Decks and outdoor furniture made with unfinished pressure-treated wood can be left untreated. I toned down the greenish tinge and the pronounced grain by applying one coat of a solid-color exterior stain.

# Victorian Toolshed

*BY ALAN AND GILL BRIDGEWATER*

This beautiful shed draws inspiration from a little out building that I loved when I was a child. The proportions of the design make a garden shed that is just right for storing your lawnmower and tools.

The toolshed comprises four primary frames (the front, back, and two sides), which are all made from 1⅜" by 2⁵⁄₃₂" (35 x 20mm) sections covered in feather-edged board. It has a steeply pitched roof sloping down at each side, a narrow door, and airholes in the gable. The decorative details are made from 6" (152.4mm)-wide boards. The floor is built directly on small-section joists, the idea being that you can mount the shed on blocks, a concrete base, or slabs. The structure is designed so that two people can easily move the component parts to the site. The interior has been left plain so it can be customized.

## Tools and Materials

- Pencil, ruler, tape measure, marking gauge, and square
- Two portable workbenches
- Crosscut saw
- Cordless electric drill with a Phillips screwdriver bit
- Twist bits to match the screw, nail, dowel, and vent hole sizes
- Small hammer
- Coping saw
- Electric jigsaw
- Small screwdriver
- Electric sander with a pack of medium-grade sandpaper
- Paintbrush: 1⁹⁄₁₆" (4cm)
- Pine, 2⁵⁄₃₂" (2cm) thick: 35 each, 1⅛" x 10' (2.9cm x 3m)
- Pine, 2⁵⁄₃₂" (2cm) thick: 6 each, 6" x 10' (15.2cm x 3m)
- Pine, 1³⁄₁₆" (3cm) thick: floor joists, 2 each 2" x 6½" (5.1 x 16.5cm)
- Pine, 2⁵⁄₃₂" (2cm) thick: 2 each, 2⁹⁄₁₆" x 10' (6.5cm x 3m)
- Pine, feather-aged board, ½" (1.3cm) thick: cladding frames, 60 each, 4" x 10' (10.2cm x 3m)
- Galvanized T-strap hinges: 3 each, 10" (25.4cm) long
- Galvanized sliding gate latch, complete with screws and coach bolts to fit
- Zinc-plated, countersunk cross-headed screws: 200 x 1½" (3.8cm) no. 8, 100 x 2" (5cm) no. 8
- Galvanized nails: 4.4 lb x ³⁄₃₂" x 1⁹⁄₁₆" (2kg x 2.4mm x 4cm)
- Roof felt: 47¼" x 11 ¹³⁄₁₆" (1.2m x 30cm)
- Acrylic paints: assorted
- Clear preservative

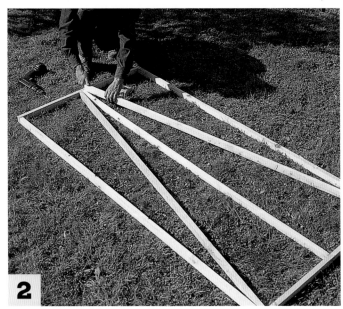

**1. Cut the wood to size.** Take the lengths of wood that make the front panel, and butt joint them with 1½" (38mm) screws. Set the two 6" (15.2cm)-wide front feature boards in place on the front of the frame (at either side of the door) and fix with 1½" (38mm) screws. Adjust for squareness. Screw the doorway battens on the back of the frame with 1½" (3.8cm) screws.

**2. Build the back frame.** Fit a central vertical flanked by two diagonal braces. Aim to make the braces fit tightly into the frame. Build two identical side panel frames complete with central, vertical, and diagonal braces, as you did for the back frame.

**3. Build the doorframe with the two sections of wood.** Use 1½" (3.8cm) screws, and 2" (5.1cm) screws for fixing the diagonal brace pieces. Make two identical roof frames, each including a roof location bar, using two 1½" (38mm) screws at each joint.

**4. Make the gable frames.** Make two identical triangular gable frames with roof support blocks positioned to make location points for the roof frames. An offcut is used to ensure that the location slot is the correct size.

**5. Position the roof.** When you have covered the gable frames by nailing on the feather-edged boards, use the coping saw to cut through the cladding to make a roof location slot, 2⁵⁄₃₂" (20mm) wide and 1⅜" (35mm) deep, on the two elevated sides of the gable triangle.

**6. Clad the other frames with feather-edged board.** Use a simple jig to ensure that the overlap of the boards is constant. Drill holes for the nails, making sure that the nail doesn't pass through an underlying feather-edged strip. Use the jigsaw to make the decorative barge boards. Sand all the panels and paint them on the outside.

Once all parts are built, assembly is a breeze.

## ASSEMBLING AND FINISHING

Set the wall panels on the base and fix with 2" (51mm) screws running into the floor joists. Locate the roof panels and screw in place with 2" (51mm) screws. Wrap felt over the join between the two roof panels and fix with nails. Use 1½" (38mm) screws to attach the ridge board on top of the felt. Screw the decorative barge boards to the front edges of the panels, and the finials to the barge boards, with 1½" (38mm) screws. Drill three vent holes in the front gable. Fit the hinge and latch. Give all surfaces a coat of preservative. The floor panel should have an extra coat on the underside and on the ends of the joists.

# Planter Bench

The idea of this popular project is sensible and simple: hang a bench seat between a pair of planter boxes. This version of the planter bench has a traditional look, and it's easy to build. Although it is made of durable materials for outdoor use, the piece will require some routine maintenance to sustain its proud good looks—and a little in-season green-thumb attention to keep the flowers blooming. The planter boxes that support the cedar bench are large enough and deep enough to support some impressive plantings. Hiding under the cedar is a pair of boxes made of pressure-treated plywood. If you are going to make

**Tools and Materials**

- Router, with beading bit, and ½" (1.2cm) roundover bit
- Saws: 7¼" (18.4cm) circular, table, miter, and saber or scroll saw
- Drill driver, with ¾" (1.9cm) spade bit
- Clamps: assorted
- Wrench
- Tape measure
- Paintbrush
- PT plywood ¾" (1.9cm): 1 sheet
- PT plywood ½" (1.3cm): 1 sheet
- Cedar (6): 1" x 4" x 10' (2.5cm x 10.2cm x 3m)
- Cedar (6): 5⁄4" x 4" x 10' (3.2cm x 10.2cm x 3m)
- Cedar (1): 5⁄4" x 4" x 10' (3.2cm x 10.2cm x 3m)
- Construction adhesive
- Screws, galvanized: 1¼" (3.2cm)
- Screws, stainless steel: ¾" (1.9cm), 1" (2.5cm), 1¼" (3.2cm), 1⅝" (4.1cm), 2½" (6.3cm)
- Screws, stainless steel finishing: 2¼" (5.7cm)
- Stainless steel carriage bolts (6): ¼" x 4" (6.3mm x 10.1cm), with nuts and washers
- Primer/sealer
- Paint: white exterior latex
- Finish: Spar varnish, solvent-based

## BUILDER'S NOTES

With this project, you don't simply park yourself on a comfortable seat in the garden; you sit in the garden. The planters will be filled with a fertile soil, of course, so you have to take this into account in choosing your materials.

**PLANTER BENCH PARTS LIST**

| | Part | Quantity | Materials | Dimensions |
|---|---|---|---|---|
| A | Box bottom | 2 | PT plywood | ¾" x 22½" x 22½" (1.9 x 57.1 x 57.1cm) |
| B | Box inner bottom | 2 | PT plywood | ½" x 21½" x 21½" (1.2 x 54.6 x 54.6cm) |
| C | Box side (front/back) | 4 | PT plywood | ½" x 14¼" x 21½" (1.2 x 36.2 x 54.6cm) |
| D | Box side (side) | 4 | PT plywood | ½" x 14¼" x 22½" (1.2 x 36.2 x 57.1cm) |
| E | Stiffener (front/back) | 4 | PT plywood | ¾" x 3½" x 21½" (1.9 x 8.9 x 54.6cm) |
| F | Stiffener (side) | 4 | PT plywood | ¾" x 3½" x 20" (1.9 x 8.9 x 50.8cm) |
| G | Wide stile | 8 | PT plywood | ¾" x 3" x 15" (1.9 x 7.6 x 38.1cm) |
| H | Narrow stile | 8 | 1x cedar | ¾" x 2¼" x 15" (1.9 x 5.7 x 38.1cm) |
| I | Top rail | 8 | 1x cedar | ¾" x 3¾" x 18" (1.9 x 9.5 x 45.7cm) |
| J | Bottom rail | 8 | 1x cedar | ¾" x 3" x 18" (1.9 x 7.6 x 45.7cm) |
| K | Feet | 8 | 5⁄4x cedar | 1" x 5" x 5" (2.5 x 12.7 x 12.7cm) |
| L | Foot molding | 32 | 1x cedar | ¾" x 4 1/4" x 4¼" (1.9 x 10.8 x 10.8cm) |
| M | Ca molding | 8 | 5⁄4x cedar | 1" x 2½" x 26¼" (2.5 x 6.3 x 66.7cm) |
| N | Cove molding | | 1x cedar | ¾" x ¾" x 25¼" (1.9 x 1.9 x 64.1cm) |
| O | Seat mounting cleat | 2 | 5⁄4x cedar | 1" x 1¾" x 18" (2.5 x 4.4 x 45.7cm) |
| P | Apron | 2 | 5⁄4x cedar | 1" x 2½" x 50" (2.5 x 6.3 x 127cm) |
| Q | Bracket | 4 | 5⁄4x cedar | 1" x 6" x 6" (2.5 x 15.2 x 15.2cm) |
| R | Seat board | 6 | 5⁄4x cedar | 1" x 3¼" x 50" (2.5 x 8.2 x 127cm) |
| S | Seat batten | 2 | 1x cedar | ¾" x 3½" x 18" (1.9 x 8.9 x 45.7cm) |

a box to hold lots of damp, rich soil, this material is the one to use because preservatives in the wood make it almost rot-proof. One obvious drawback is its appearance. To address that, you can use paint. After you construct the boxes, but before you apply the cedar trim, paint the plywood to conceal the greenish color, and four small painted panels on each planter box are all you'll see in the completed project. The project is modular, so you can easily alter the length of your bench. Another option is to link several boxes with benches, and even use the assemblies to turn a corner on a deck. And if all you want is a planter without a bench, this may be your project, too. Just make the planter box.

## MATERIALS

The USDA Forest Products Laboratory show that pressure-treated wood rated for ground contact won't rot even after 40 years. That's why I selected pressure-treated plywood for the planter boxes. But bear in mind you need to protect yourself while you work. The chemical treatment can spread in sawdust when you make cuts. So you need a good dust mask and a workable plan for capturing and properly disposing of the sawdust and scraps. (Don't burn them.)

I used cedar to dress up the planters and make the bench. It's attractive, weathers well, and is easy to work. I used stainless-steel screws to eliminate stains. (The galvanized screws are only for assembling the plywood boxes.)

I used finishing screws to attach the cap moldings.

## TOOLS AND TECHNIQUES

Quite a bit of the stock for this project needs to be ripped to widths other than those that are lumberyard standards.

To make the feet, you need a beading bit for your router. It's like a round-over bit, except that the pilot bearing is undersized, so the cutter forms a step at the bearing-end of the quarter-round profile.

The roundover bit (a ½" radius) comes into play a few steps further on, when you need to nose the edges of some seat boards. Here, the complete cut takes two passes, one with the router on the top surface of the board, the second with the router on the bottom surface. Each pass removes stock from half the board thickness. On the first pass, the pilot rides along the lower half of the board's edge as the cutter shapes the upper half. When you turn the board over, you discover the bearing doesn't have a reference surface. It's been cut away. What to do? Use a router accessory called an edge guide.

## FINISH

For the outsides of the plywood boxes, I used ordinary white latex house paint. I applied two full-strength coats after sealing the knots and priming. I finished all the cedar with solvent-based marine spar varnish, which is more durable than its water-based counterpart.

## CUTTING BOX PANELS

Under their cedar duds, the planter boxes are really nothing more than butt-jointed plywood boxes. Working within the caveats that apply to using pressure-treated wood, cut the plywood. (Remember, you should use eye protection and a dust mask to guard against the sawdust that is laden with wood-preservative chemicals.) Set out a pair of sawhorses, and lay scrap 2x4s or furring strips across them. Then lay the plywood on top. You can strike a line and follow it freehand using your circular saw. But to ensure straight cuts, it's a good idea to use a straightedge.

Cut the parts to the dimensions specified on the cutting list, noting that the list assumes you are making two boxes. If you plan to make a two-bench unit, you have to make at least three boxes. Again, you should feel free to alter my basic plans if you want to customize the piece to suit your needs.

When you make the cuts, first check the depth of cut on your saw. You'll find that if you adjust the blade to cut just slightly deeper than the plywood, you can cut efficiently. And if you choose to use a support under the cut line, the blade will barely cut into it. After completing the cuts, sweep up and bag the sawdust for disposal. (Remember, you should not burn sawdust or small scraps of pressure-treated lumber in a fireplace or woodstove.)

## DRAINAGE HOLES

The two-piece bottom consists of a ½" plywood panel centered on the slightly larger ¾" piece. This creates a ½"-wide rabbet for the sides to sit in. Apply a bead of adhesive around the perimeter of the smaller piece and center it on the larger one. (You can use a scrap of ½" plywood as a gauge to make sure the top piece is centered all the way around.) Then apply three or four clamps. Turn the assembly over, and drive several galvanized decking screws through the underside to fasten the panels together.

Working on the top side, lay out a grid for locating the drainage holes. Draw three lines parallel with each side, making them 3" apart. At each intersection, drill a ¾"-diameter hole all the way through the bottom assembly. I used a spade bit for this job. Again, wear a dust mask, and sweep up and bag the wood chips for disposal.

## ASSEMBLING THE BOXES

Join the four sides of the boxes using butt joints. Use the two identical bottom pieces as assembly forms when fastening the sides. With a clamp holding three sides of the box in the forms, apply adhesive to the appropriate edges of the fourth side, and fasten it with screws or nails. After the sides of both boxes are joined, install a bottom in each one.

You may find that the sides of the boxes are bowed a bit. To counter the bowing, cut strips of ¾" plywood (stiffeners), and glue and screw them to the insides of the boxes. Orient each strip so that its bow is opposite to that of the side.

After the boxes are assembled, prime and paint. I recommend latex for both the primer and paint. You don't need to coat the insides of the boxes.

## FACE FRAMES

Construct the frames with butt joints between the stiles and rails and at the corners between the two adjoining stiles. The stiles you'll apply to the front and rear faces are 3" wide. Those applied to the ends are 2¼" wide, and when combined with the edges of the adjoining stiles, they form a 3"-wide surface. The best way to construct the frames is to cut and join the stiles, forming corner assemblies. Apply the corners

to the boxes; then cut the rails to fit, and attach them. All the stiles should be 15" long, extending from the bottom edge of the box to the top edge. Crosscut the stiles from 1x4 stock, and then rip half of them down to 2¼" wide and the other half to 3" wide.

To form each corner assembly, glue a narrow stile to a wide one, edge to face, using construction adhesive. Clamp the assemblies, and set them aside over-night. (Be careful that you don't dent the soft cedar when you clamp these corner boards; use small scraps of wood to protect the wood from the clamps.) Sand the completed corners; then glue and screw them to the planter boxes. Apply beads of adhesive to the back of a corner, press it into place, and align it; then clamp it temporarily. Drive three or four stainless-steel screws through pilot holes in the plywood and into the back of each stile.

After you've attached all the stiles, measure and cut the rails. The top rails are partially covered by the cove molding, so you can use 1x4 stock and set the rails ¼" down from the top of the plywood. The bottom rails are 3" wide. Glue and screw them in place as you did the stiles.

## MAKING FEET

Each foot is a two-ply construction glued and screwed to the bottom of the planter. The bottom layer is simply a 5"-square piece of 5/4 cedar. The top layer is a 4½" square of one-by cedar. All edges get a quarter-round bead using a router and ¾" beading bit.

Cut the eight blocks needed for the bottom layer of the foot assemblies. Hold off on crosscutting the upper layer. Routing pieces this small can be tricky with a hand-held router. First, rip a 36" board to the desired width: 4¼". Rout the profile on the long edges of this board and across both ends as well. Make a small-workpiece holder about a foot long with three nails driven through it in a triangular pattern at one end. The points of the nails should protrude about ⅜ inch. Tack a fence across the board about 3½"–4" from one end. Clamp this fixture to your workbench so that the nail end is right at or slightly over the edge.

Crosscut the first two blocks from each end of your working strip. They should be 4¼" square with a routed profile on three edges. Take one, and press it down on the nails, orienting the piece so that you can rout the fourth edge. The router will hold the workpiece down, and the nails will prevent it from twisting. To avoid splinters, work in from both edges, and end the cut in the center. Crosscut the other two blocks from the working strip. You'll need to route the profile on two sides of these blocks.

Make the feet by bonding a top and bottom section together with adhesive. Then stick them to the planters at the corners. Drive a couple of screws through the planter into the foot and a couple through the foot into the planter.

## MAKING CAP MOLDING

The cap molding is attached to the top edge of the planter box to finish it. It covers the plywood edges as well as the edges of the frame pieces. Rip the cap stock to the width specified on the cutting list. Check the dimensions of your planter, and adjust the cap molding as needed. (The molding should overlap the inner face of the box by ⅛".) As you crosscut the pieces, miter the ends.

It's wise to test-fit the pieces on your benchtop (without glue), and check the fit of the miter joints. You want tight-fitting miters, even if that means the unit is slightly out of square. When the assembly looks right, attach it to the top of the planter box. Apply adhesive to the top edges of the planter box, and press the strips in place. There are many things you can do to get tight miter joints (aside from making accurate cuts), and one of the most important is using clamps. Just be sure that the clamp surfaces don't mar your wood. Lastly, drive three or four stainless-steel finishing screws through each molding piece into the top edges of the planter.

## MAKING COVE MOLDING

Cove molding fits under the cap to trim the planter. The molding is ⅝" wide and ¾" high, shaped with a ½" cove bit. Rout the profile on the edge of a wide board; then rip off the strip. To produce the right amount, crosscut two or three 28"-long boards. Rout the profile on the two long edges, rip off the ⅝"-wide molding, and rout and rip again. Cut the strips to fit, mitering the ends, and glue and screw them in place. I used three ¾"-long 6-gauge stainless-steel screws in

each strip, and drilled and countersunk pilot holes so that the slender molding wouldn't split.

## CUTTING BENCH PARTS

The bench has six seat boards, two aprons, two mounting cleats, and four brackets made from 5/4 stock. Two seat battens are cut from one-by stock. Rip and crosscut all these parts except two of the seat boards to the cutting-list dimensions. The outer two seat boards are nosed along one edge. You can rout this profile in two passes with a roundover bit, using an edge guide to control the second cut. Without a guide for the second cut, the bit's pilot bearing will ride on the roundover profile you've already cut and produce a different profile on the second side of the board. You need to hold off on cutting these two boards so that you can clamp them for the routing operation. After nosing the edges, you can rip and crosscut the boards to final size.

## SHAPING BRACKETS

The four brackets are 6" x 6" with a 5½"-radius arc. For maximum strength you'll want to shape them so the grain of the wood runs diagonally. To this end start by making a 45-degree cut on one end of a length of 5/4 x 6 stock. Make a template of hardboard or MDF and use it to guide the arc cut. Make the template by cutting a piece of ½" MDF or ¼" hardboard to the dimensions indicated in the drawing. Using a router and trammel, cut the arc and trim down the template to 6" wide, leaving it at the 12" length. To use the template, align it to the 45 degree cut you made, then clamp the template and the workpiece to your workbench with the area to be cut overhanging the edge. Scribe along the bottom edge of the template on the stock, and mark along the tiny flat at the tip of the arc as well. Using a saber saw, cut close to the edge of the template; then trim the bracket edge to match the template using a pattern bit in your router.

After all four brackets have been partially shaped, square them. Then swing the miter saw back to 0. Nip the tip of the arc on each bracket. Measure 6" from that tip, and square a cut line across the bracket to finish.

## MOUNTING CLEATS

Before you incorporate the cleats into the bench assembly, bore three holes for the mounting bolts, and use them as templates for drilling matching holes in the planter boxes. The cleats will overlay the top rail on the planter box frames, with the ends flush with the seam between rails and stiles. Lay a strip of 5/4 stock to represent the thickness of the seat boards on top of the mounting cleat, and set it against the rail with the scrap tight against the cove molding. When you have each hole started, remove the cleat, and extend each hole through the box side. It's a good idea to label matching cleats and planters during this stage.

## BUILDING THE BENCH

The bench is composed of the seat boards, cleats, mounting cleats, aprons, and brackets. The seat boards are joined by the seat battens and mounting cleats. The brackets are attached to the aprons, and the aprons to the seat assembly.

Lay out the six seat boards with the nosed edge on the outsides with $\frac{1}{16}$" gaps between boards. I used spacers, aligned the ends of the boards, and applied a couple of clamps. Set the two seat battens in place, and mark around them, positioning each one $6\frac{1}{2}$" from the center of the seat board length. Remove the battens, apply dots of adhesive to the seat boards inside the marks, and replace the battens. Drill pilot holes, and drive $1\frac{1}{4}$" stainless steel screws into the seat boards.

Glue and screw the mounting cleats to the seat. I used $2\frac{1}{4}$" finishing screws to secure the cleats, driving them in pilots with $\frac{1}{2}$"-deep counterbores. Be sure you orient the cleats with the appropriate faces out, so you can align them with the holes you drilled in the boxes.

Next, attach the brackets to the aprons. The brackets are positioned flush with the ends of the aprons and are inset about $\frac{1}{8}$" from the face to create a shadow line at the seam. Fasten them using adhesive and one $2\frac{1}{4}$" finishing screw and one $1\frac{5}{8}$" screw. The long screw is driven through the apron into the bracket. You need to drill at least a 1" counterbore so that a $2\frac{1}{4}$" screw will penetrate the bracket. Drive the short screw through the edge of the bracket into the apron.

Lastly, join the apron-and-bracket assemblies to the seat assembly. Use construction adhesive and six screws driven though the bottom edges of the aprons into the seat boards, and a single screw driven on an angle through the face of each cleat into the back of the apron.

Drill and counterbore pilot holes, and run a bead of adhesive on the top edge of the apron and onto the ends of the cleats. Set the apron, flush up the ends, and snug it against the seat and the ends of the cleats with clamps. Drive the screws. After you've installed both aprons, the bench is ready for a test-assembly.

## ASSEMBLING THE PLANTER BENCH

Prepare the planters by sliding a 4" carriage bolt through each hole in the planter. The heads should be inside the planter. Fit one end of the bench into the projecting bolt shanks. Get just one bolt all the way through into its hole in the cleat, and you are on your way. That one bolt will support one end of the bench, allowing you to support the other end while you slide the second planter into final position.

Once the bench is well supported, focus on fine adjustments that lead to getting all the bolts pushed through the planter and the mounting cleat. Slip a washer over the bolt shank, thread the nuts, and tighten.

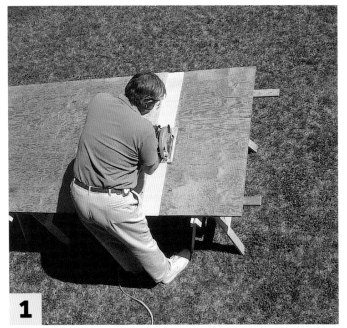

**1. Support the complete sheet on 2x4s or furring strips that are laid across a pair of sawhorses.** This is necessary when you break down large sheets of plywood into smaller pieces for the planter-box panels.

**2. Set the blade on your saw to cut just through the box panel, and you will barely kerf the support.** With this approach, the main sheet and the cut section will be supported as you cut.

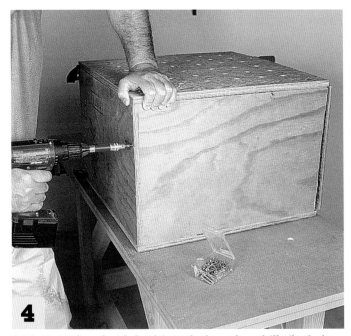

**3. Use a clamp to pull opposite sides into the rabbets formed when you glued up the bottom panels, and against the vertical edges of the third side.** Then apply adhesive to the appropriate edges of the fourth side.

**4. Work the fourth side back into the box, then drill pilot holes and drive screws to lock the parts together.** Repeat the process on the other side of the box, then use the bottom panels as forms to make another box.

**5. Glue and screw 3/4" stiffeners around the inside of the box to reduce bowing.** If the planter box side bows out, as it does here, orient any bow in the stiffener in the opposite direction.

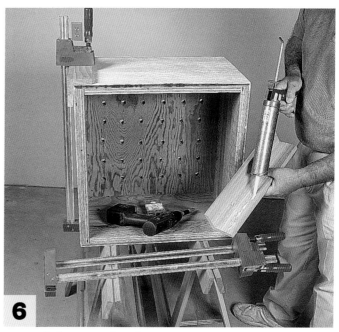

**6. Attach the corner face-frame assemblies in pairs.** Run adhesive on the backs, set them in place, clamp the assemblies tight, and drive stainless steel screws through the box sides into the backs of the assemblies.

**7. Hold the small feet pieces for routing by pressing them onto a trio of exposed nail points.** The router holds the soft cedar on the nails, which keep the block from kicking out from under the tool.

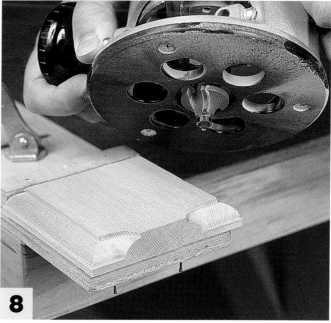

**8. Work the router from the corners towards the middle of the foot.** If you rout from corner to corner when cutting an edge profile, the bit tends to blow out splinters as it exits the wood.

**9. Apply adhesive to the mitered ends and the planter box's top edges to get tight miter joints on the cap molding.** Fit the section in place and screw through the edge of one molding piece into the adjoining piece.

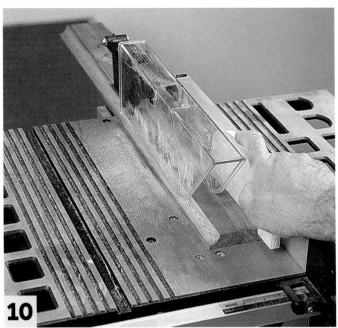

**10. Rout the cove molding profile on both edges of a board.** Then, rip the molding from the board. You can make molding from scraps of stock if the pieces are long enough and have knot-free edges.

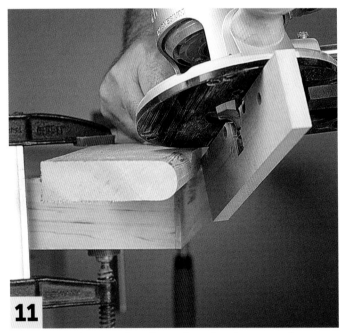

**11. Bullnose the outer bench seat boards using a roundover bit and an edge guide.** When the pilot bearing hangs below the quarter-round profile on the second pass, the guide orients the bit correctly.

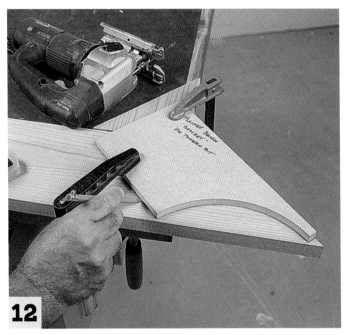

**12. Shape brackets by aligning the bracket template with the mitered end of the stock to rout the arc.** Use several clamps (set free of the router path) to secure the work so that it won't chatter under the cutting action.

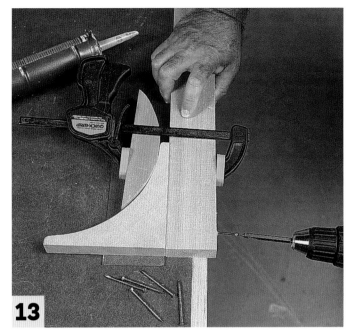

13. **With the apron flat on your bench and the bracket on a scrap of ⅛" hardboard to create the offset, predrill through the edge of the apron.** Then, drive a long stainless-steel screw into the bracket.

14. **Assemble the bench by locking the bench to the planters one bolt at a time.** With one bolt in place, you can align the bulky assembly to insert the other bolts through the planter into the bench mounting cleat.

## FINISHING

I finished the planter bench with marine spar varnish. After cleaning off all the beads of squeezed-out adhesive using a chisel and utility knife, do whatever touch-up sanding seems appropriate. Use a shop vacuum and a tack cloth to mop up every bit of sanding dust.

Following the manufacturer's directions, apply the finish. In most cases, you should apply a slightly thinned first coat, followed by two full-strength top coats. I allowed each coat to dry at least one day and sanded lightly between applications.

# Classic Arbor

*BY ALAN AND GILL BRIDGEWATER*

This project is built around four slender lattice screens. Buy the screens first, as you may only be able to obtain them in a slightly different size to what we have quoted, and make adjustments to other materials if necessary. Basically, the arbor is a seat for two enclosed on three sides, with a roof over the top. We have designed the project so that it can be made as six knockdown units—the two lattice sides, the back panel, the two roof panels, and the seat—with various other pieces used to support and decorate. The feather-edged boards are lapped in such a way that they channel rain off the roof and back panel. The strength and stability of the overall structure are guaranteed by diagonal braces fixed to both the back panel and the roof. When we went to purchase the materials, the only available lattice screens and 6" (150 mm) boards were pre-treated with rather heavy brown wood preservative, so we decided to lift the design by leaving all the other components in their natural color.

## Tools and Materials

- Pencil, ruler, tape measure, compass, bevel gauge, and square
- Two portable workbenches
- Cordless electric drill with a cross-point screwdriver bit
- Selection of drill bits to match screw sizes
- Crosscut saw
- Hammer
- Four large clamps
- Electric jigsaw
- Electric sander with a pack of medium-grade sandpaper
- Paintbrush: 1 9/16" (4cm)
- Lattice screens: 4 screens, 72" (1.83m) x 12" (30.3cm) (sides)
- Pine: 4 pieces, each 6½' (2m) long, 3" x 3" (7.5 x 7.5cm) square section (main posts)
- Pine: 15 pieces, each 10' (3m) long, 2" (5cm) wide, and 1¼" (3.2cm) thick (roof and back panels, seat supports, and A-brace)
- Pine: 6 pieces, each 10' (3m) long, 6" (15cm) wide, and ⅞" (2.2cm) thick (top and bottom side boards, seat, decorative barge boards)
- Pine feather-edged board: 20 pieces, each 10' (3m) long, 4" (10cm) wide, and 1 3/32" (1cm) thick (back panel and roof)
- Zinc-plated, countersunk cross-headed screws: 100 x 2" (5cm) no. 8, 100 x 2 23/64" (6cm) no. 10, 20 x 3½" (8.9cm) no. 10
- Galvanized wire nails: 2.2 lb (1 kg) 1 9/16" (4cm) x 3/32" (2.6mm)
- Clear preservative

**1. Sandwich the lattice screens between the main posts and screw them in place with 2" (5cm) screws.** Set a 6" (15cm)-wide board at top and bottom and screw these to the posts with 2" (5cm) screws. Rerun this procedure so that you have two identical side panels.

**2. Use the 2" x 1 ¼" (5cm x 3.2cm) section to make the back frame.** Cut the parts to size with the crosscut saw and fix them with 2 ²³⁄₆₄" (6cm) screws. Screw blocks of waste at the angles to help firm up the joints.

**3. Cut the feather-edged board into 39" (1m) lengths and position these on the back frame so that they lap over from top to bottom.** This will ensure that rain will be thrown off the back of the arbor. Drill pilot holes and fix the strips to the frame with the 1⁹⁄₁₆" (4cm) nails.

**4. Clamp the two side panels to the back panel and fix with the 2 ²³⁄₆₄" (6cm) screws.** Drive the screws through the edges of the panel and into the posts. Check the structure for squareness and then add the additional horizontal and diagonal braces to the back panel.

**5. Position and fit the base for the seat, and then build off the seat to make the backrest.** Fit the seat support battens with 2" (5cm) screws. Use the jigsaw to cut the 3" (7.5cm) radius curves on the top of the backrest boards. Leave a $^{25}/_{32}$" (2cm) space between the boards on both the seat and the backrest.

**6. Build and clad the two roof panels in much the same way as the back panel.** Then fix additional strengtheners in place with 2 $^{23}/_{64}$" (6cm) screws—a diagonal brace, a drip batten, and a location brace (see the working drawing).

**7. Set the two roof panels in place so that the location batten is more or less centered on the post (at all four corners).** Then, fix with the 3½" (8.9cm) screws. Run the screws up at an angle, with at least two screws for each post.

**8. With 2" (5cm) screws, fix the A-brace to link the two roof panels.** Draw the shape of the barge boards and fret them out with the jigsaw. Clamp the boards in place and fix with 2" (5cm) screws. Fit the finial spike to cover the joint. Finally, sand everything to a splinter-free finish and give the arbor a coat of preservative.

# Adirondack Chair

*BY DANA AND MICHAEL VAN PELT*

This Adirondack chair was inspired by the work of Charles and Henry Greene, influential early 20th-Century American architects, whose style featured organic lines and understated accents. Where straight, hard lines are found in a traditional Adirondack chair, such as on the arms, legs, and stretchers, we employed slight curves to better reflect the Greene brothers' aesthetic. Many Adirondack chair arm supports and legs stand flat and perpendicular to the seat and lounging leg. We modified this approach by rotating the front leg 90° to the lounging leg, giving the arm extra strength where it grasps the leg.

We decided to use mahogany hardwood. You could choose another material if you prefer, but keep in mind this is an outdoor project that will be subject to the elements. Lyptus, a hybrid lumber, would work well, as would teak—just be sure that it's plantation grown. We would recommend avoiding cedar and redwood, but cypress would be a nice softwood alternative.

Enlarge the patterns to full-size, and make hardboard or plywood templates of the pieces for best results. Then, transfer the shapes to your stock by tracing around the templates with a pencil. And be sure to save the templates, in case you wish to make additional chairs.

The chair's back slats were inspired by a garden gate at a home designed by Charles and Henry Greene.

## BEGINNING THE FOUNDATION

Start by making the arms (A). Trace the arm pattern onto the stock with a pencil, and then lay out the stopped dado on its lower face. Before you shape this piece on the band saw, mill the stopped dado using a router and a ¾" (19mm)-dia. straight bit. Use a clamped-on straightedge to guide your cut.

Then, mill the back arm support and the front legs (B and C). Note that the arm support has one 30-degree edge. After transferring these shapes to the wood, cut out their forms—along with the arms that you started above—on the band saw. Sand the edges smooth with a spindle sander. A drum sander chucked into a drill press would also work

Cut out the side lounging legs (D). The notch that fits into the front leg should be part of the template. Lay out the three router-made, ¾" (1.9cm)-wide openings on each leg. The two long, parallel cuts are decorative. The short cut is actually a mortise made to accept the under brace (E). Machine the under brace, forming the tenons with a dado head installed in your table saw; use a miter gauge and a registration block clamped to your fence. Then, with a sharp chisel, carefully round over the tenons to match the router-made through mortises, testing the fit as you go.

Smooth the edges of the legs and back arm support with sandpaper, moving up progressively through the grits until you reach 500. Then round over the top and bottom edges of the arms

Some of the cloud lifts and curves require cutting tight corners on the band saw.

with a ¼" (6mm)-dia. roundover bit. Assemble these pieces using wood glue and screws. Counterbore the exposed screws, and then glue plugs into the counterbored holes, with the exception of those on

A spindle sander smooths edges, removes saw marks, and helps shape some of the curves.

the arms. Clamp a support to the back arm support to hold it in its appropriate position until the back slats are added.

The next step is to make the rear and front cross slats (F and G). Note that the rear slat has a 20° front edge. Mark their patterns, cut them to shape, and sand off the saw marks. Attach the front cross slat with screws in counterbored holes, and then plug the counterbored holes.

Locate the position of the rear cross slat by clamping two straight guide boards to the front edge of the back arm support. The boards should be long enough to rest on the under brace. Place the rear cross slat in its approximate position on top of the lounging legs, and then slide it forward until it touches the guide boards. With the arms square to the front legs, the two angled faces of the back arm support, and the rear cross slat flat to the guide boards, you will

A trim router equipped with a roundover bit adds emphasis to the chair's soft organic shapes.

find the proper location for the cross slat. Later in the assembly, the back slats will occupy the space where the guide boards are during this step.

Attach the rear cross slat with screws in counterbored holes, and plug the counterbored holes.

## MAKING THE REMAINING SLATS

Make all seven seat slats (H). Attach all but the one closest to the rear cross slat. Set that piece aside for now. Secure the rest of the slats with screws in counterbored holes, and plug the counterbored holes.

While the back looks as if it is made from three pieces of stock, it is actually assembled from five separate pieces (I through K). Cut and shape the back slats as you did the earlier pieces, and glue the narrow and center back slats together using wood glue. Then, chuck a ¼" (6mm)-dia. roundover bit in your router, and round over the appropriate edges of the back slats. Test-fit the back slats. They should stand on top of the under brace, just as the guides did earlier. Make any necessary adjustments.

Next, make the back top brace (L). Then, fasten the back slats to the back top brace and to the back arm support with screws in counterbored holes. Note that the screws driven through the front face of the back slats should be drilled in the decorative pattern shown in the drawings on page 123. Plug the three counterbored holes on the face of the back top brace.

Attach the final seat slat as you did the others. It should touch the back slats.

## ADDING DETAILS AND FINISH

Using the sharp chisel, chop shallow square mortises at each of the decoratively drilled screw holes and the exposed screw holes on the arms. Mix black (ebony) two-part epoxy, and fill the mortises you just formed. Allow the epoxy to cure.

Sand up through all the grits, taking your time, and then apply several coats of teak or other exterior oil finish. Reapply this finish yearly to keep the wood fresh.

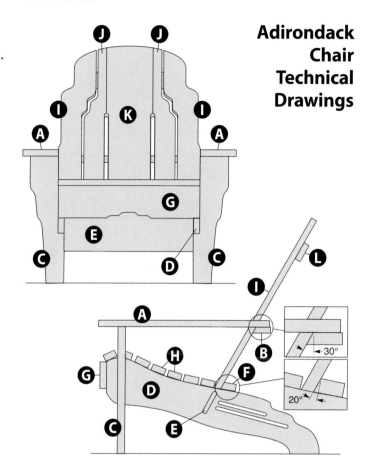

**Adirondack Chair Technical Drawings**

| ADIRONDACK CHAIR PARTS LIST | | | |
|---|---|---|---|
| | Part | Quantity | Dimensions |
| A | Arms | 2 | 1" (2.5cm) x 6" (15.2cm) x 30½" (77.5cm) |
| B | Back Arm Support | 1 | 1" (2.5cm) x 3" (7.6cm) x 30" (76.2cm) |
| C | Front Legs | 2 | 1" (2.5cm) x 6" (15.2cm) x 21½" (54.6cm) |
| D | Side Lounging Legs | 2 | 1" (2.5cm) x 12" (30.5cm) x 40" (101.6cm) |
| E | Under Brace | 1 | 1" (2.5cm) x 6" (15.2cm) x 25" (63.5cm) |
| F | Rear Cross Slat | 1 | 1" (2.5cm) x 2½" (6.4cm) x 25" (63.5cm) |
| G | Front Cross Slat | 1 | 1" (2.5cm) x 4½" (11.4cm) x 25" (63.5cm) |
| H | Seat Slats | 7 | 1" (2.5cm) x 2½" (6.4cm) x 25" (63.5cm) |
| I | Back Outside Slats | 2 | 1" (2.5cm) x 8" (20.3cm) x 31¾" (80.7cm) |
| J | Back Narrow Slats | 2 | 1" (2.5cm) x 4" (10.1cm) x 32¾" (83.2cm) |
| K | Back Center Slat | 1 | 1" (2.5cm) x 8" (20.3cm) x 32¾" (83.1cm) |
| L | Back Top Brace | 1 | 1" (2.5cm) x 3¼" (8.3cm) x 19" (48.3cm) |

# Plans

## Stylish Birdhouse

### Chip Carving Pattern

Enlarge 175%

# Stylish Birdhouse

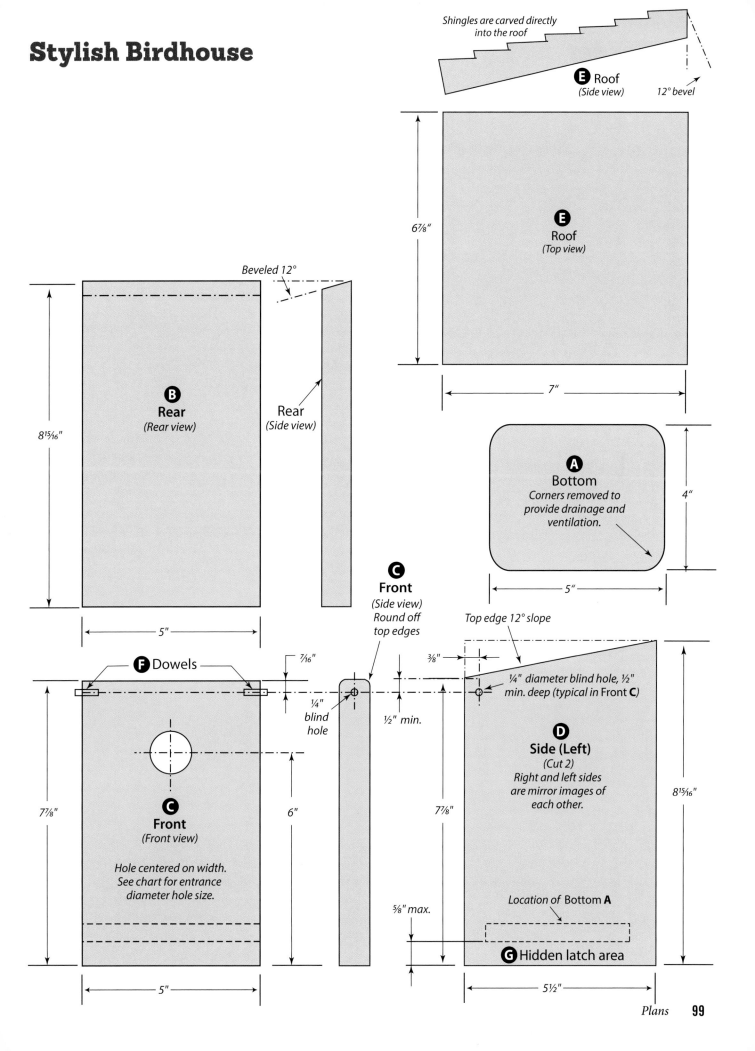

*Shingles are carved directly into the roof*

**E** Roof
*(Side view)*

*12° bevel*

**E** Roof
*(Top view)*

6⁷⁄₈"

7"

Beveled 12°

**B**
**Rear**
*(Rear view)*

Rear
*(Side view)*

8¹⁵⁄₁₆"

5"

**A**
Bottom
*Corners removed to provide drainage and ventilation.*

4"

5"

**C**
**Front**
*(Side view)*
Round off top edges

*Top edge 12° slope*

**F** Dowels

7⁄₁₆"

³⁄₈"

¼" diameter blind hole, ½" min. deep (typical in Front **C**)

¼"
blind
hole

½" min.

**C**
**Front**
*(Front view)*

*Hole centered on width. See chart for entrance diameter hole size.*

7⁷⁄₈"

6"

**D**
**Side (Left)**
*(Cut 2)*
*Right and left sides are mirror images of each other.*

7⁷⁄₈"

8¹⁵⁄₁₆"

*Location of Bottom* **A**

⅝" max.

**G** Hidden latch area

5"

5½"

# Bird Feeder

Enlarge 105%

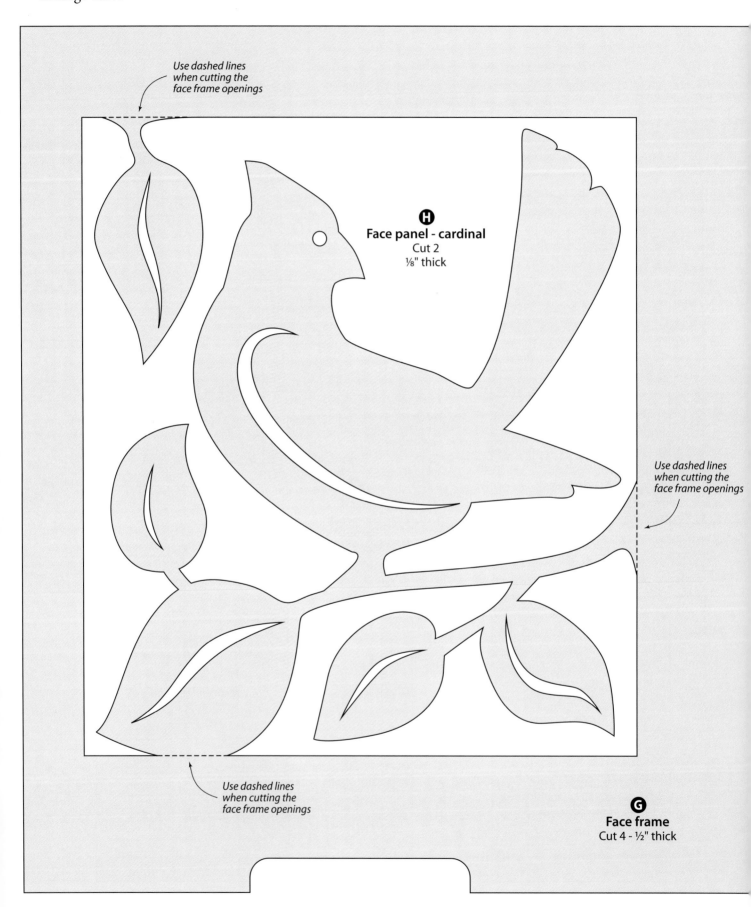

Use dashed lines when cutting the face frame openings

**Face panel - cardinal**
Cut 2
⅛" thick

Use dashed lines when cutting the face frame openings

Use dashed lines when cutting the face frame openings

**Face frame**
Cut 4 - ½" thick

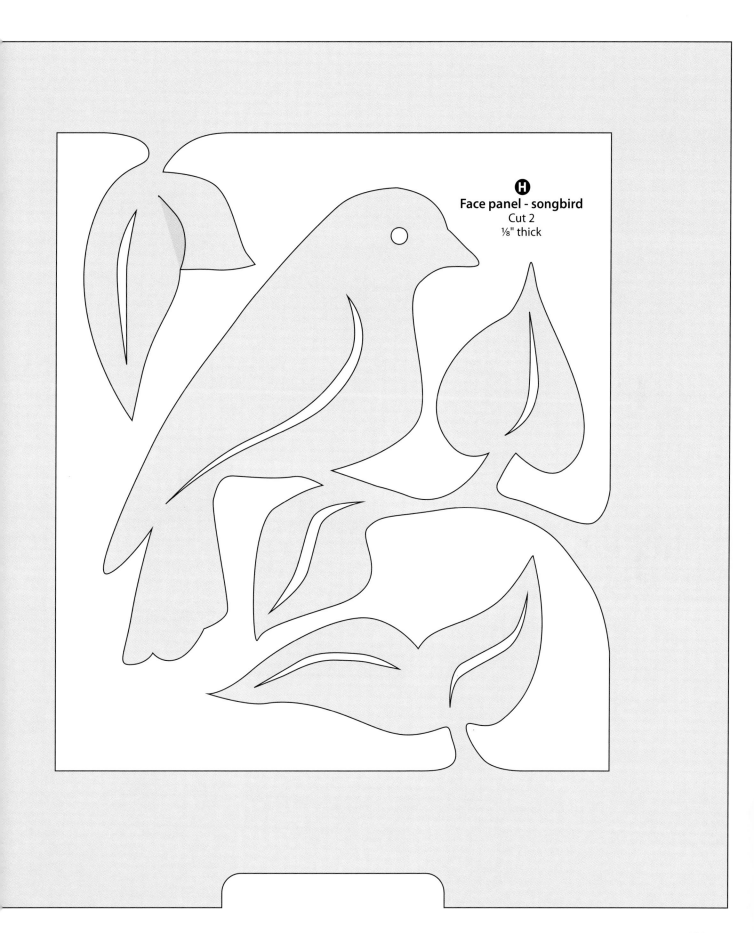

**Face panel - songbird**
Cut 2
⅛" thick

# Bird Feeder Pattern

Enlarge 200%

**A**

**Section support**
Cut 2 – ½" thick

Cut center slots to thickness of the wood. One support has a top slot, and the other a bottom slot.

Cut a 45° bevel to the front and back sides of the support

Bottom view

# Bird Feeder Pattern

Enlarge 200%

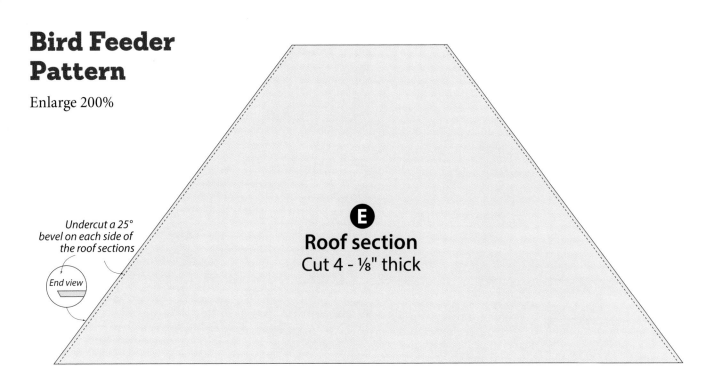

*Undercut a 25° bevel on each side of the roof sections*

End view

## E
## Roof section
Cut 4 - ⅛" thick

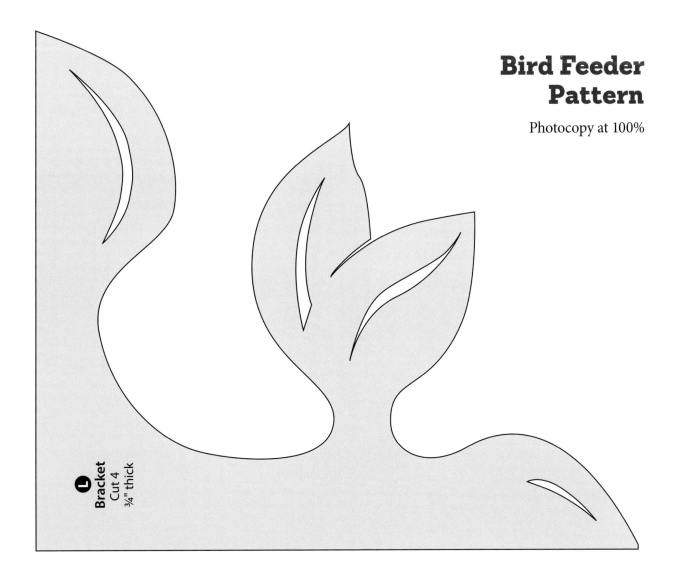

# Bird Feeder Pattern

Photocopy at 100%

## L
**Bracket**
Cut 4
¾" thick

# Bat Box Measured Drawings

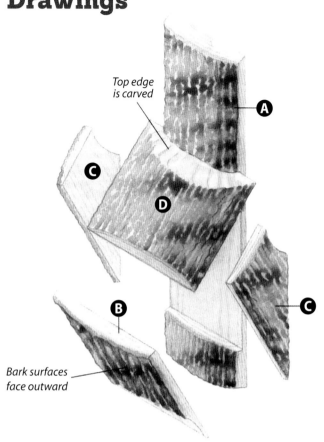

Top edge is carved

Bark surfaces face outward

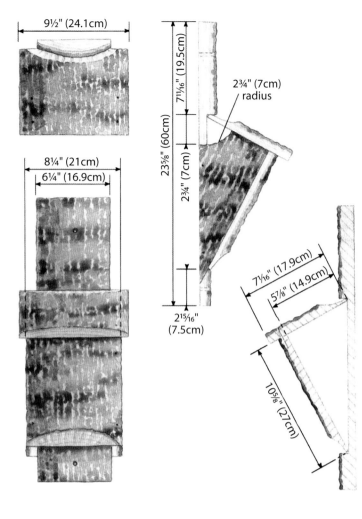

9½" (24.1cm)

8¼" (21cm)

6¼" (16.9cm)

2¹⁵⁄₁₆" (7.5cm)

7¹¹⁄₁₆" (19.5cm)

23⅝" (60cm)

2¾" (7cm)

2¾" (7cm) radius

7¹⁄₁₆" (17.9cm)

5⅞" (14.9cm)

10⅝" (27cm)

# Japanese Birdbath Measured Drawings

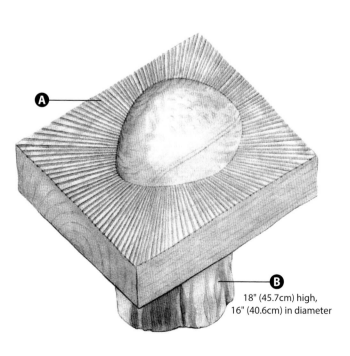

18" (45.7cm) high, 16" (40.6cm) in diameter

## Top View

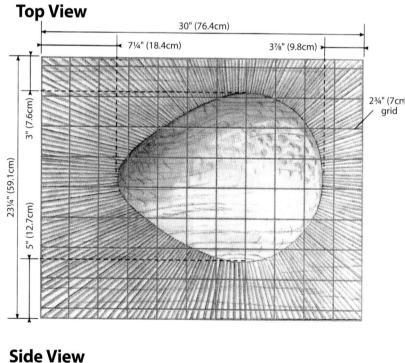

30" (76.4cm)

7¼" (18.4cm)

3⅞" (9.8cm)

3" (7.6cm)

23¼" (59.1cm)

5" (12.7cm)

2¾" (7cm) grid

## Side View

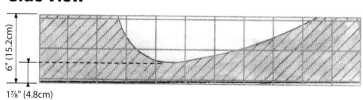

6" (15.2cm)

1⅞" (4.8cm)

# Backyard Dominoes
## Dot Pattern

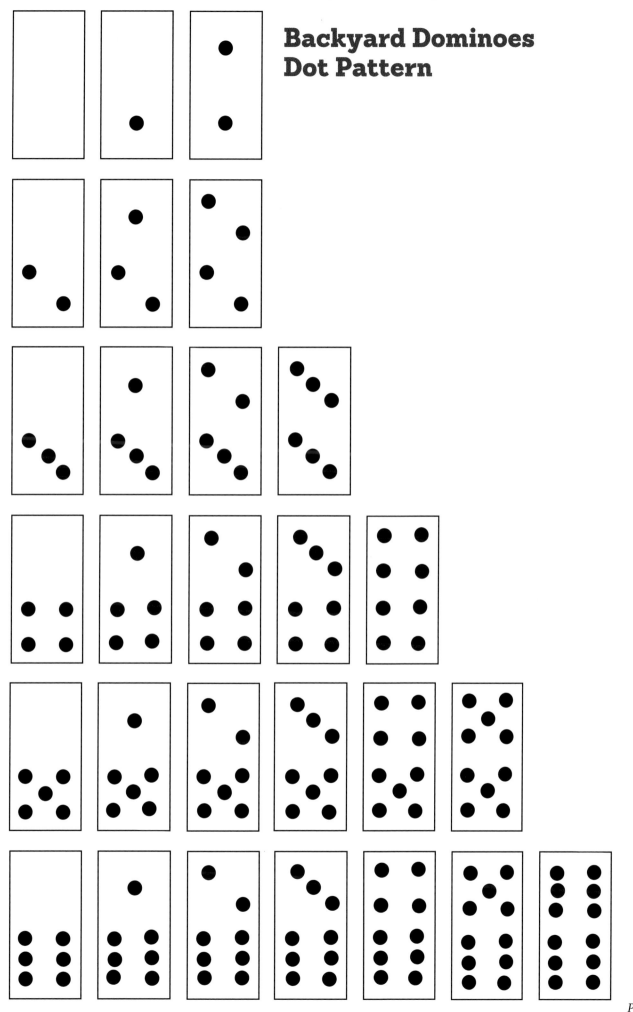

# Gnome Door Pattern

Photocopy at 100%

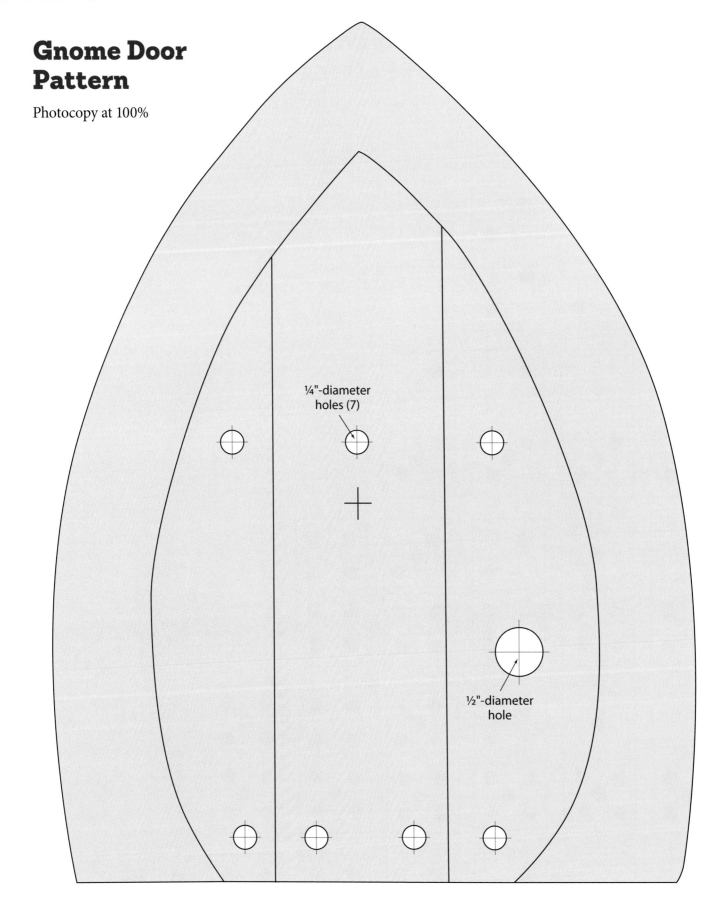

¼"-diameter
holes (7)

½"-diameter
hole

# Lyrical Herb
# Box Patterns

Photocopy at 100%

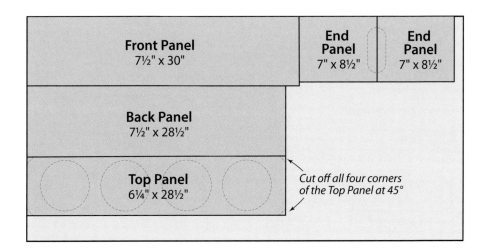

Front Panel
7½" x 30"

End Panel
7" x 8½"

End Panel
7" x 8½"

Back Panel
7½" x 28½"

Top Panel
6¼" x 28½"

*Cut off all four corners of the Top Panel at 45°*

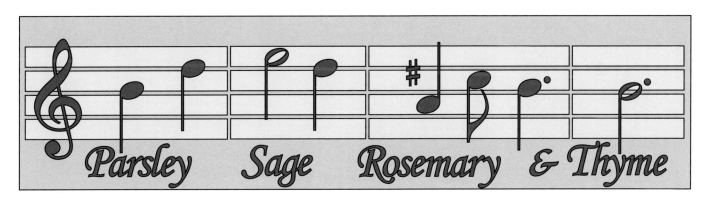

Parsley    Sage    Rosemary    & Thyme

Slats are positioned 1¼" from the top

| 9" Slats | 6" Slats | 9" Slats | 5" Slats |
|---|---|---|---|

# Lyrical Herb Box Patterns

Photocopy at 100%

# Lyrical Herb Box Patterns

Photocopy at 100%

# Lyrical Herb Box Patterns

Photocopy at 100%

*Lavender*

*Oregano*

*Basil Mint*

*Chives*

# Lyrical Herb Box Patterns

Photocopy at 100%

# Rainwater Harvester

## Measured Drawing

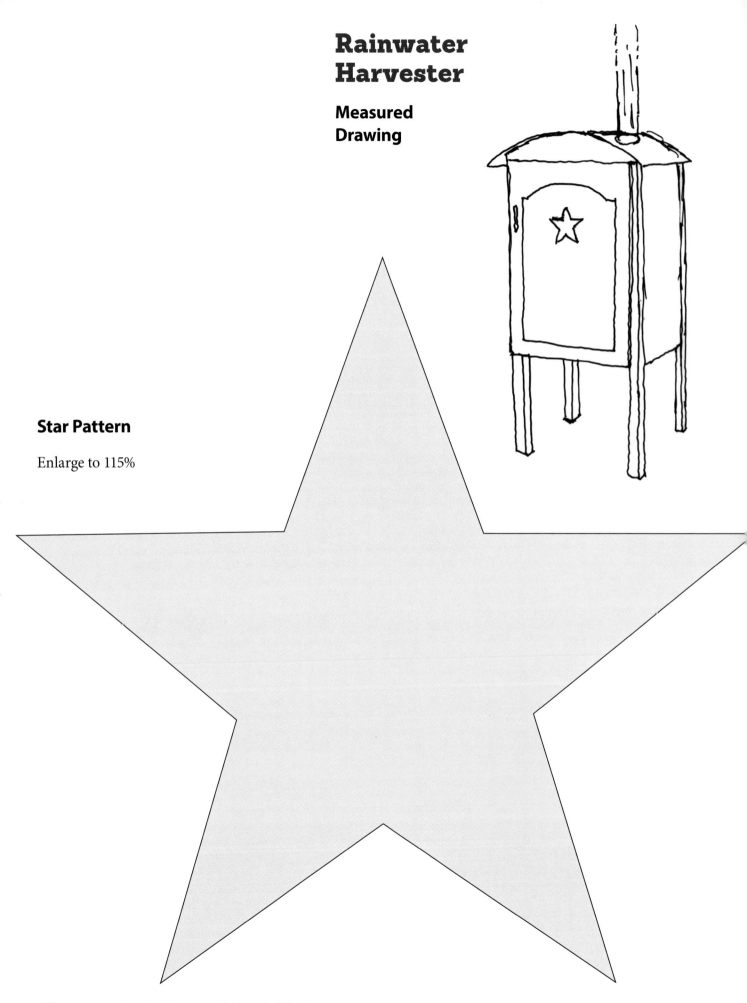

## Star Pattern

Enlarge to 115%

# Hammock Stand

## Exploded View

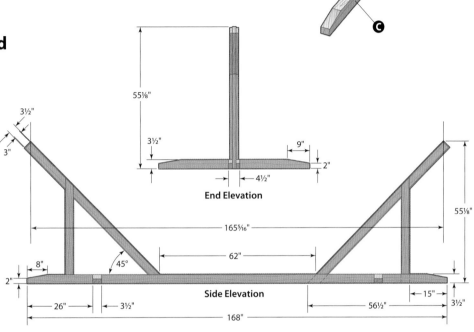

## Hammock Stand Elevations

55⅛"

3½"

End Elevation

3½"

3"

55⅛"

165⁵⁄₁₆"

62"

45°

8"

9"

2"

4½"

2"

26"

3½"

Side Elevation

56½"

15"

3½"

168"

## Hammock Stand Parts

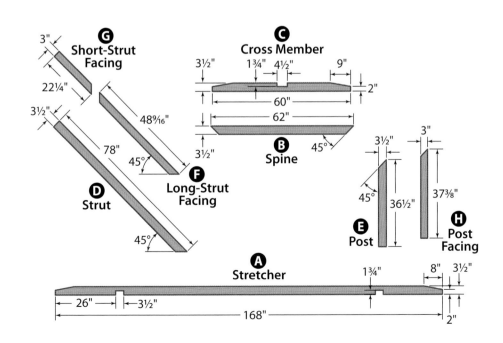

**G** Short-Strut Facing
3"
22¼"

**C** Cross Member
3½"  1¾"  4½"  9"
2"
60"
62"
45°
3½"

48⁹⁄₁₆"
3½"
78"
45°

**B** Spine

**F** Long-Strut Facing

**D** Strut
45°

**E** Post
3½"
45°
36½"

**H** Post Facing
3"
37⅜"

**A** Stretcher
26"  3½"
1¾"  8"  3½"
168"
2"

# Victorian Toolshed

## Front Panel - *Front view*

**Ledge**
²⁵⁄₃₂" x 2⁹⁄₁₆" x 21³⁄₁₆"
(2cm x 6.5cm x 53.8cm)

Dimensions
back pane

**Brace**
²⁵⁄₃₂" x 2⁹⁄₁₆" x 21⁵⁄₃₂"
(2cm x 6.5cm x 85.1cm)
55° ends

**Front Feature Board**
²⁵⁄₃₂" x 6" x 74 ¹³⁄₃₂"
(2cm x 15cm x 1.89m)

**Front Frame**
²⁵⁄₃₂" x 1³⁄₈" x 70⁷⁄₈"
(2cm x 3.5cm x 1.8m)

**Brace**
Same as above

**Doorway Batten**
²⁵⁄₃₂" x 1³⁄₈" x 80¹³⁄₁₆"
(2cm x 3.5cm x 2.053m)
45° top

**Front frame**
²⁵⁄₃₂" x 1³⁄₈" x 35"
(2cm x 3.5cm x 88.8cm)

(Doorframe underneath doorway batten)

## Back Panel - *Back view*

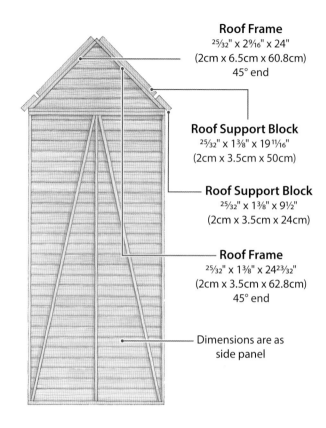

**Roof Frame**
²⁵⁄₃₂" x 2⁹⁄₁₆" x 24"
(2cm x 6.5cm x 60.8cm)
45° end

**Roof Support Block**
²⁵⁄₃₂" x 1³⁄₈" x 19¹¹⁄₁₆"
(2cm x 3.5cm x 50cm)

**Roof Support Block**
²⁵⁄₃₂" x 1³⁄₈" x 9½"
(2cm x 3.5cm x 24cm)

**Roof Frame**
²⁵⁄₃₂" x 1³⁄₈" x 24²³⁄₃₂"
(2cm x 3.5cm x 62.8cm)
45° end

Dimensions are as
side panel

## Side Panel - *Inside view*

²⁵⁄₃₂" x 1³⁄₈" x 35"
(2cm x 3.5cm x 88.8cm)

**Cladding**
½" x 4" x 35"
(1.3cm x 10cm x 88.8cm)

**Central Vertical Brace**
²⁵⁄₃₂" x 1³⁄₈" x 70⁷⁄₈"
(2cm x 3.5cm x 1.8m)

**Diagonal Brace**
²⁵⁄₃₂" x 1³⁄₈" x 72¹¹⁄₁₆"
(2cm x 3.5cm x 1.846m)
78° ends

½" x 1³⁄₈" x 35"
(1.3cm x 3.5cm x 88.8cm)

## Roof Panel
*Inside view*

**Roof Frame**
²⁵⁄₃₂" x 1³⁄₈" x 45¾"
(2cm x 3.5cm x 1.15m)

**Feather-Edged Board**
½" x 4" x 46²⁷⁄₃₂"
(1.3cm x 10cm x 1.19m)

**Roof Frame**
²⁵⁄₃₂" x 1³⁄₈" x 31½"
(2cm x 3.5cm x 80cm)

**Roof Location Bar**
²⁵⁄₃₂" x 1³⁄₈" x 45¾"
(2cm x 3.5cm x 1.15m)

²⁵⁄₃₂" x 1³⁄₈" x 45¾"
(2cm x 3.5cm x 1.15m)

## Floor Panel - *Underside*

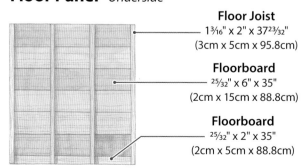

**Floor Joist**
1³⁄₁₆" x 2" x 37²³⁄₃₂"
(3cm x 5cm x 95.8cm)

**Floorboard**
²⁵⁄₃₂" x 6" x 35"
(2cm x 15cm x 88.8cm)

**Floorboard**
²⁵⁄₃₂" x 2" x 35"
(2cm x 5cm x 88.8cm)

## Side View

**Finial**
$^{25}/_{32}$" x 5$^1/_8$" x 13 $^{25}/_{32}$"
(2cm x 13cm x 35cm)

1 grid square equals 2" (5cm)

**Decorative Barge Board**
$^{25}/_{32}$" x 5$^1/_8$" x 13 $^{25}/_{32}$"
(2cm x 13cm x 35cm)

1 grid square equals 2" (5cm)

**Cross-Section of the Roof Ridge Boards**

$^1/_2$" x 4" x 46$^{27}/_{32}$"
(1.3cm x 10cm x 1.19m)
(cladding)

$^{25}/_{32}$" x 1$^3/_8$" x 46$^{27}/_{32}$"
(2cm x 3.5cm x 1.19m)

## Exploded View

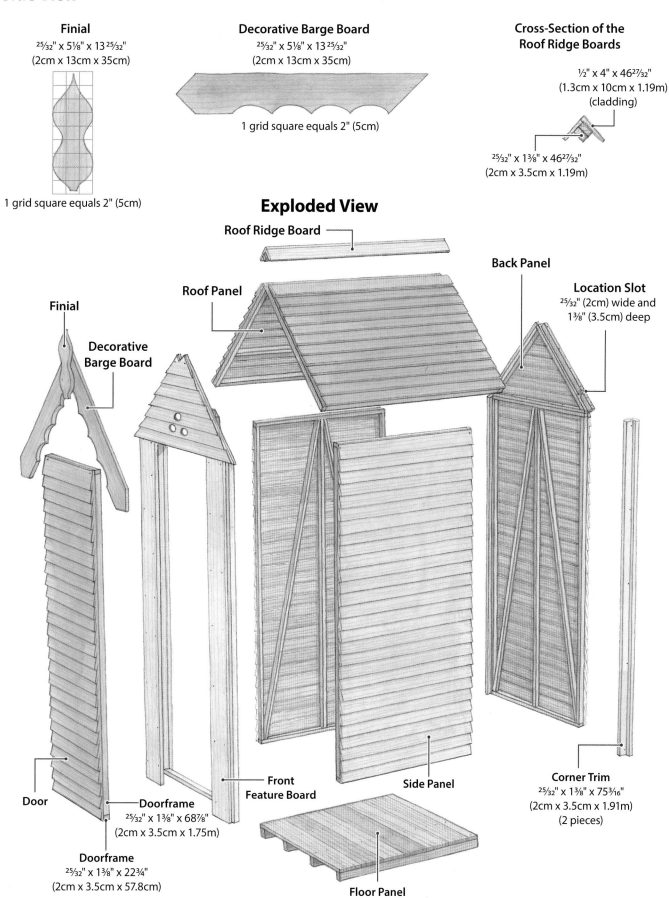

**Roof Ridge Board**

**Back Panel**

**Location Slot**
$^{25}/_{32}$" (2cm) wide and
1$^3/_8$" (3.5cm) deep

**Roof Panel**

**Finial**

**Decorative Barge Board**

**Door**

**Doorframe**
$^{25}/_{32}$" x 1$^3/_8$" x 68$^7/_8$"
(2cm x 3.5cm x 1.75m)

**Doorframe**
$^{25}/_{32}$" x 1$^3/_8$" x 22$^3/_4$"
(2cm x 3.5cm x 57.8cm)

**Front Feature Board**

**Side Panel**

**Floor Panel**

**Corner Trim**
$^{25}/_{32}$" x 1$^3/_8$" x 75$^3/_{16}$"
(2cm x 3.5cm x 1.91m)
(2 pieces)

# Planter Bench

## Exploded View

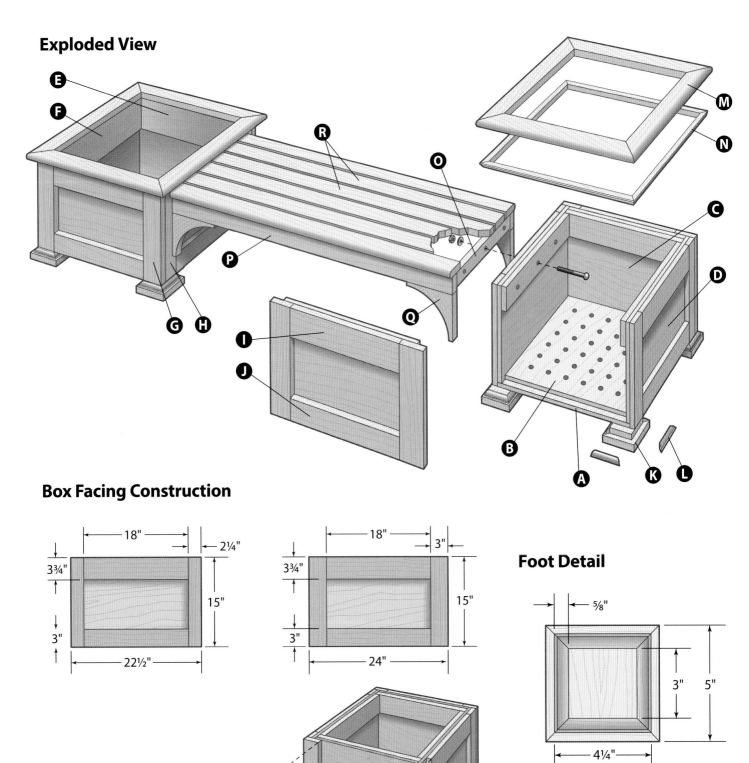

## Box Facing Construction

18"

2¼"

3¾"

15"

3"

22½"

18"

3"

3¾"

15"

3"

24"

## Foot Detail

⅝"

3"

5"

4¼"

4¼"

¾"

1"

5"

# Bench Construction

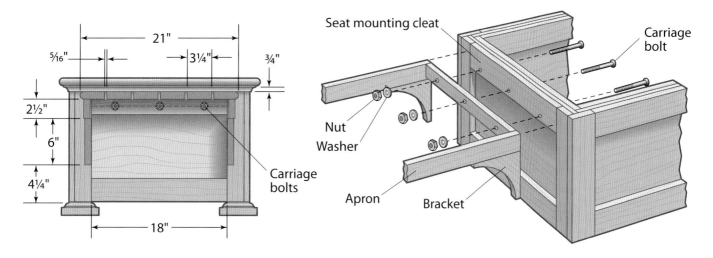

# Box Construction

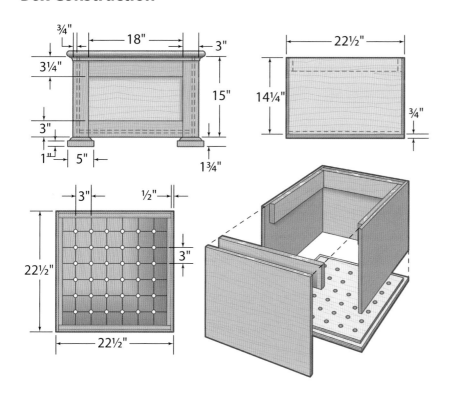

# Bracket Template

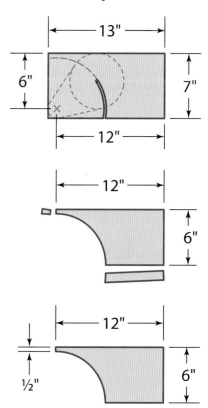

# Classic Arbor

## Side View

**Seat Support**
1¼" x 2" x 42½"
(3.2cm x 5cm x 1.08m)
Top face positioned
39" (1m) from the base

**Seat Support**
1¼" x 2" x 42½"
(3.2cm x 5cm x 1.08m)
Top face positioned
16" (40cm) from the base

**Seat Support**
1¼" x 2" x 42½"
(3.2cm x 5cm x 1.08m)
Top face positioned
11¹³⁄₁₆" (30cm) from the base

**Seat Support**
1¼" x 2" x 42½"
(3.2cm x 5cm x 1.08m)
Front face positioned
7⅞" (20cm) from the back of the seat planks

# Exploded View

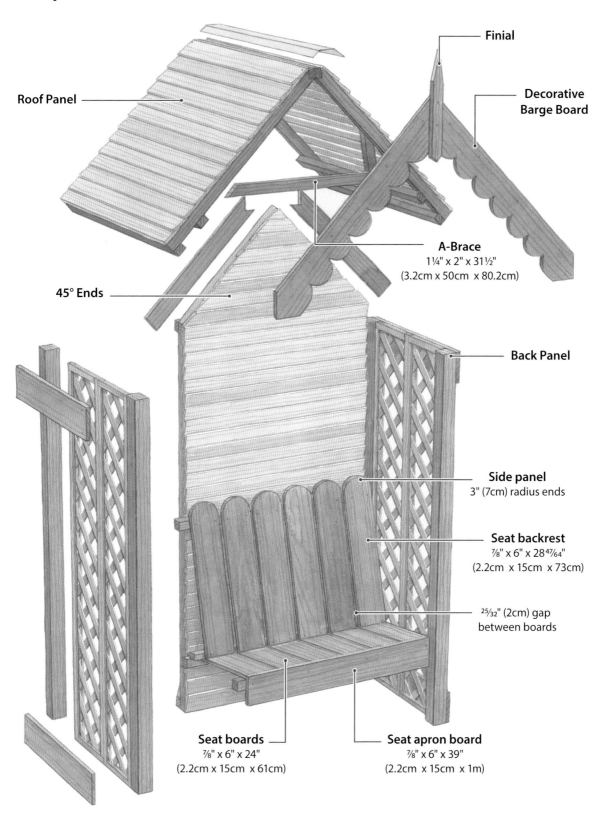

Roof Panel

Finial

Decorative Barge Board

45° Ends

A-Brace
1¼" x 2" x 31½"
(3.2cm x 50cm x 80.2cm)

Back Panel

Side panel
3" (7cm) radius ends

Seat backrest
⅞" x 6" x 28⁴⁷⁄₆₄"
(2.2cm x 15cm x 73cm)

²⁵⁄₃₂" (2cm) gap
between boards

Seat boards
⅞" x 6" x 24"
(2.2cm x 15cm x 61cm)

Seat apron board
⅞" x 6" x 39"
(2.2cm x 15cm x 1m)

# Classic Arbor

## Roof Panel
*Underside view*

1¼" x 2" x 42⅛"
(3.2cm x 5cm x 1.07m)

**Diagonal Brace**
1¼" x 2" x 33⁵⁄₁₆"
(3.2cm x 5cm x 84.6cm)
45° ends

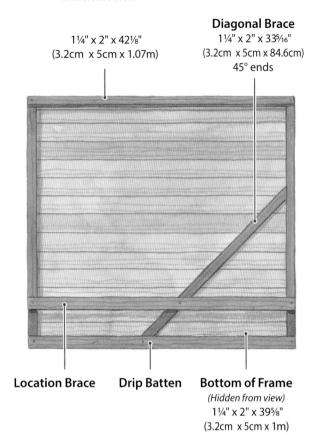

**Location Brace**  **Drip Batten**  **Bottom of Frame**
*(Hidden from view)*
1¼" x 2" x 39⅝"
(3.2cm x 5cm x 1m)

## Side Panel
*Front view*

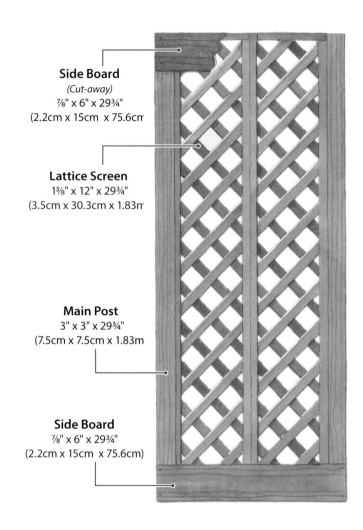

**Side Board**
*(Cut-away)*
⅞" x 6" x 29¾"
(2.2cm x 15cm x 75.6cm)

**Lattice Screen**
1⅜" x 12" x 29¾"
(3.5cm x 30.3cm x 1.83m)

**Main Post**
3" x 3" x 29¾"
(7.5cm x 7.5cm x 1.83m)

**Side Board**
⅞" x 6" x 29¾"
(2.2cm x 15cm x 75.6cm)

## Roof Panel
*Side view*

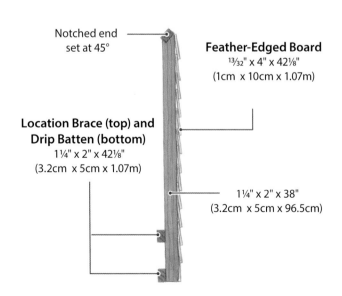

Notched end
set at 45°

**Feather-Edged Board**
13⁄32" x 4" x 42⅛"
(1cm x 10cm x 1.07m)

**Location Brace (top) and
Drip Batten (bottom)**
1¼" x 2" x 42⅛"
(3.2cm x 5cm x 1.07m)

1¼" x 2" x 38"
(3.2cm x 5cm x 96.5cm)

## Barge Board
*Front view*

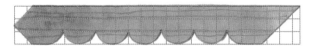

⅞" x 6" x 44½" (2.2cm x 15cm x 1.131m)
1 grid square equals 2" (5cm)
45° ends

## Finial
*Front view*

⅞" x 2" x 17 23⁄32"
(2.2cm x 5cm x 45cm)
1 grid square equals 2" (5cm)

# Back Panel
*Back view*

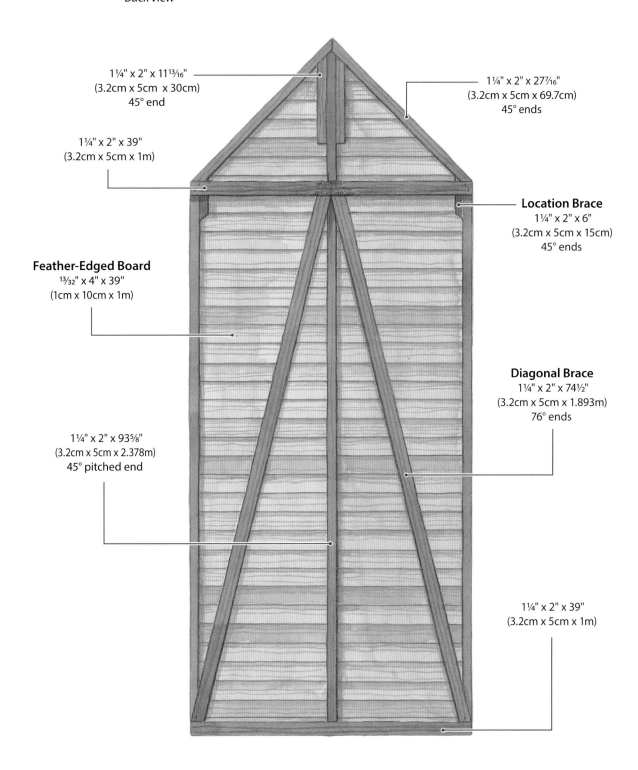

1¼" x 2" x 11¹³⁄₁₆"
(3.2cm x 5cm  x 30cm)
45° end

1¼" x 2" x 27⁷⁄₁₆"
(3.2cm x 5cm x 69.7cm)
45° ends

1¼" x 2" x 39"
(3.2cm x 5cm x 1m)

**Location Brace**
1¼" x 2" x 6"
(3.2cm x 5cm x 15cm)
45° ends

**Feather-Edged Board**
¹³⁄₃₂" x 4" x 39"
(1cm x 10cm x 1m)

**Diagonal Brace**
1¼" x 2" x 74½"
(3.2cm x 5cm x 1.893m)
76° ends

1¼" x 2" x 93⁵⁄₈"
(3.2cm x 5cm x 2.378m)
45° pitched end

1¼" x 2" x 39"
(3.2cm x 5cm x 1m)

# Adirondack Chair

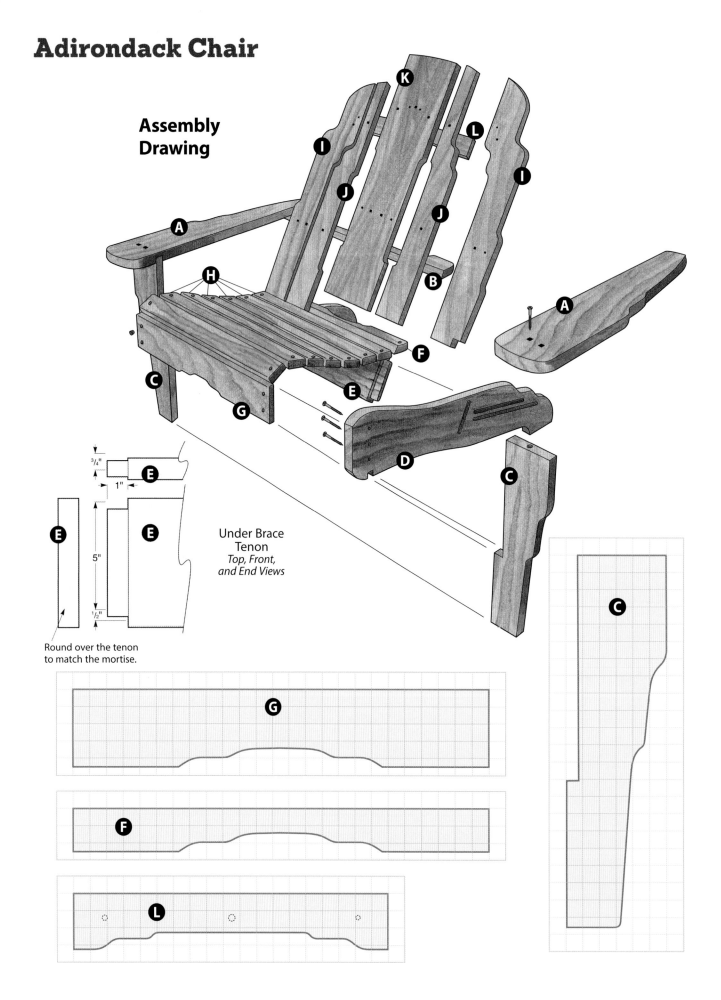

**Assembly Drawing**

Under Brace
Tenon
*Top, Front,
and End Views*

¾"
1"
5"
½"

Round over the tenon
to match the mortise.

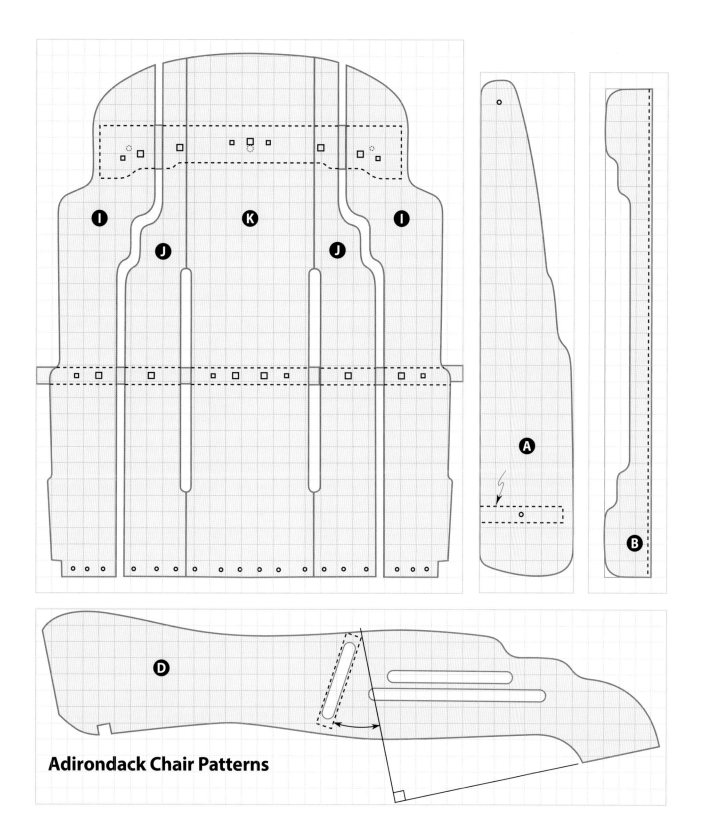

**Adirondack Chair Patterns**

# Index

Note: Page numbers in *italics* indicate projects and plans/drawings (in parentheses). Page numbers in **bold** indicate authors' bios.

# About the Authors

Alan and Gill Bridgewater have gained an international reputation as promoters of the self-sufficient lifestyle. They produce gardening, woodworking, and DIY books on a range of subjects, including furniture-making, hand tool techniques, stone and brickwork, decks and decking, wood-carving and woodturning. They have written more than 50 highly successful books to date, including *The Self-Sufficiency Specialist* and *The Wildlife Garden Specialist*. Alan and Gill frequently contribute articles and designs to national magazines.

A lifelong designer and woodcrafter, Jon Deck was the art director of *Woodcarving Illustrated* and *Scroll Saw Woodworking & Crafts* magazines for over 20 years.

Frank Egholm lives in Denmark, where he taught woodworking in a school for several years. He's the author of *Snitte: The Danish Art of Whittling: Make Beautiful Wooden Birds* and *The Danish Art of Whittling: Simple Projects for the Home*. He's also organizing an annual "Snittefest" whittling festival in Denmark. His wife Lillian has illustrated most of Frank's books, as well as a few of her own. She also photographs parts of Frank's books. For more of his work, visit his website at snittesiden.dk.

Chris Gleason is the author of several books for the DIY market including *Built-In Furniture for the Home, The Complete Kitchen Makeover, Complete Custom Closet, Old-School Workshop Accessories,* and *Building Real Furniture for Everyday Life*. He was raised on a farm in upstate New York. He has been raising chickens in his Salt Lake City backyard for over six years. He currently builds and sells chicken coops. He has owned Gleason Woodworking Studios for over 13 years.

Barry Gross is a popular author and instructor on the subject of turning. His book *Pen Turner's Workbook* is available from Fox Chapel Publishing. For more of his work, visit *bgartforms.com*.

Nick Hamilton is a trained horticulturist and the owner of Barnsdale Gardens, Britain's largest collection of individually designed gardens, with 38 working gardens on an eight-acre site. He carries on the legacy of his father, the late Geoff Hamilton, legendary host of the BBC's *Gardener's World* TV show. Nick is the author of *The Barnsdale Handy Gardener, Geoff Hamilton—A Gardening Legend,* and *Grow Organic*. He has a lifelong passion and enthusiasm for organic gardening, principles that he puts into practice at Barnsdale Gardens.

Bill Hylton is the author of *Router Magic* and *Woodworking with the Router*, and appears at woodworking seminars and demonstrations around the country. He is an expert on routers, power tools, and furniture building. He lives in Quarryville, Pennsylvania.

Mike McGrath is editor-at-large for Organic Gardening and is the former editor-in-chief. He writes a monthly column, "Mike McGrath's Tall Tales," and answers questions on the magazine's website. McGrath's "You Bet Your Garden" airs weekly on National Public Radio. He has made frequent guest appearances on NBC's Weekend Today and NPR's "All Things Considered."

Barry McKenzie is a popular instructor and owner of the School of Chip Carving. He has several instructional and pattern booklets available. Barry also writes a regular chip carving newsletter. Visit him online at chipcarvingschool.com.

Paul Meisel has had 10 years' experience as an industrial arts instructor. He now owns Meisel Hardware Specialties, a project plan and woodworking supply company that focuses on distributing plans for woodworking projects that are accessible for carving students and beginners as well as experts.

Stephen Moss is a naturalist, author, and TV producer. His TV credits include *Springwatch, Birds Britannia,* and *Britain's Big Wildlife Revival,* and his books include *Wild Hares and Hummingbirds, A Bird in the Bush,* and *Tweet of the Day.* He has traveled to all seven continents to film and write about wildlife. Stephen is one of Great Britain's top nature writers with a monthly column in *The Guardian.* He also writes for the *Daily Mail, Daily Telegraph,* and magazines including Birdwatch, and *BBC Wildlife.*

Colleen Pastoor is the owner and creator of the popular DIY blog *Lemon Thistle,* where she shares DIY, home décor, and hand lettering ideas and tutorials. Colleen also teaches workshops in person and online. She has been featured in *Country Sampler, Better Homes & Gardens, Redbook, Today's Parent Magazine, Buzzfeed,* and *Country Living Online.* To learn more about Colleen and her work, visit her website (LemonThistle.com), YouTube channel, Instagram (@ColleenPastoor), or Facebook page (@LemonThistleBlog).

The late Ojars Plisis lived in Cambridge, Wis.